PROPERTY OF THE JCC IN MANHATTAN
334 AMSTERDAM AVENUE NY, NY 10023

GOD IS PROOF ENOUGH

by Walter S. Wurzburger

Devora Publishing

Published by Devora Publishing
Text Copyright © 2000 by Walter S. Wurzburger

All rights reserved. No part of this book may be reproduced or transmitted in any form or by any means, electronic or mechanical, including photo-copying, recording, or by any information storage and retrieval system, without permission in writing from the publisher.

Design: Tiffen Studios (Chaim Mazo)
Cover Design: Ben Gasner

Devora Publishing books may be purchased for educational or special sales by contacting:

Marketing Director, Devora Publishing
40 East 78th Street, Suite 16D
New York, New York 10021
Tel: 1-800-232-2931
Fax: (212) 472-6253
E-mail: pop@netvision.net.il

ISBN: 0-943706-80-7

Printed in Israel

Contents

Acknowledgments 5
Introduction 7

The Human Self 11
Beyond Autonomy 18
The Search For Meaning And Purpose 26
God-Centeredness Versus Self-Centeredness 33
The Role of Arguments For The Existence of God 39
Sex, Love And Family 50
The Covenant And The Uniqueness Of The Jewish Experience 57
Faith And History 61
The Problem Of Evil And The Holocaust 67
Cultivation Of Faith 76
Human Initiatives And Messianic Redemption 85
Walking The Middle Ground 93
Jewish Responsibility To The World 99
Integrating Opposing Values Into The Service Of God 104
The Sabbath: A Model Of Integration 109
The Quest For God And The Emulation Of His Ethical Attributes .. 116
The Never-Ending Search 122

Sources And Bibliography 124

Acknowledgments

This book grew out of numerous experiences acquired in fifty years as a pulpit Rabbi as well as twenty six years of teaching philosophy and Jewish thought at Yeshiva University.

Many of the positions articulated in the forthcoming pages reflect the inspiration and impact of my revered teacher and mentor, HaRav Joseph B. Soloveitchik of blessed memory.

Some of the ideas in this book appeared in my writings in various journals and scholarly publications. I thank Yeshiva University Press, The Jewish Publication Society of America, The Cross Road Publishing Company, *Tradition*, Kluwer Academic Publishers, Commission of Synagogue Relations of the Federation of Jewish Philanthropies of New York, and *The Journal of Jewish Communal Service* for permission to republish from my writings.

I also want to record my gratitude for the encouragements and the many helpful suggestions I received from my friend, Rabbi Reuven Bulka, who read the complete draft of an early manuscript.

But above all I want to thank my beloved Naomi not only for her invaluable input into the formulation of my ideas but for creating an atmosphere that makes my intellectual pursuits possible.

Walter S. Wurzburger

Introduction

The idea for this book came to me when I reflected upon the amazing reply I received from a Christian student of theology whom I attempted to dissuade from converting to Judaism.

Appealing to her rather extensive knowledge of Jewish texts, I asked her:

> *"Why take such a drastic step as to embrace Judaism? You are fully aware that, according to Jewish belief, there is no need for this, because the pious of all nations are assured of a share in the World-To-Come."*

Her answer gave me a new insight into the meaning of my religious heritage:

> *"I know that. But I do not want to wait for the hereafter; I want the World-To-Come in the here and now."*

This encounter with an outsider made me realize how, as an insider, I was unable to fully appreciate what precious treasures I possessed in my religious tradition. It occurred to me that many fellow Jews could also fail to appreciate how much Jewish religious faith could contribute to the meaningfulness and worthwhileness of their existence.

The purpose of this book is to show that, while the validity of a religious faith is beyond rational proof or disproof, its profession remains a live option even for the most tough-minded.

I am fully aware, however, that the belief that religious faith would enhance the meaningfulness of our existence cannot serve as an adequate rational ground for adherence to a religion. Genuine faith cannot be founded on mere wishful thinking. The existence of a need is no proof that there is something available to satisfy this need.

When William James, American psychologist and philosopher, defended the "rationality" of religious belief on the grounds that it would render life more meaningful, critics argued that the title of his book "The Will to Believe"[1] was a misnomer. It should have been "The Will to Make Believe."

We may question whether, in light of James' adherence to a pragmatic theory of truth, this criticism can be sustained. But we must nonetheless be wary of a purely functional approach to religion, which essentially amounts to treating God as a useful fiction. Perhaps this is why the Jewish liturgy stipulates that immediately after reciting the *Shema* – the proclamation of our monotheistic belief in the absolute unity of God – we pronounce a blessing which states that what we have affirmed is true. Only afterwards do we add a number of other descriptions such as "established, correct, enduring, right, reliable, beloved, delightful... good and beautiful is this affirmation for us forever."[2]

The sequence of the attributes is significant. We do not begin with extolling the beauty, goodness or utility of what we have proclaimed. Our first and foremost concern is its *truth*. All other considerations are secondary. We cannot place our faith in fictions, no matter how useful, appealing, or attractive they may be.

Voltaire once said, "If there were no God, we would have to invent one." But it does not make sense to worship a god whom we have invented because of our need to believe in something. We would find ourselves in the ludicrous position of the apocryphal clergyman who prayed "Oh God, if there is one, save my soul, if I've got one!"

It, therefore, will not do to simply postulate the existence of God in order to avoid our human life being reduced to meaninglessness or absurdity. According to the *Talmud*, "Truth is the seal of the Holy One, Blessed be He."[3] In the words of the Psalmist, "God is near to those who call upon Him," but only if "they call upon Him in truthfulness." Appealing fictions spun by wishful thinking cannot provide a solid foundation for religious faith.

In the final analysis, since the human mind is not equipped to tackle a metaphysical issue such as the existence of God, the decision for or against religious faith is not a matter that can be settled by any kind of objective evidence. In the absence of any rational necessity, it is left to free human beings to make an existential choice. This choice will, in large measure, determine into what kind of selves we wish to *make* ourselves.

THE HUMAN SELF

ONE OF THE HALLMARKS OF MODERNITY is the belief that personal autonomy is the pivot which supports the entire structure of ethical obligation and responsibility.

The emphasis on individual autonomy, with its focus upon self-determination, downplays the social dimension of morality. We take it for granted that each human being should govern his or her conduct in accordance with what the individual believes to be right or good. Regardless of whether these beliefs are grounded in reason or sentiment or whether they represent purely arbitrary decisions, morality is conceived as revolving around the dictates of the subjective, autonomous conscience.

Whereas the ethos of antiquity and the Middle Ages stressed the responsibilities devolving upon individuals as members of society, the modern era has witnessed a radical transformation of the nature of ethical obligation. The growing emphasis upon individualism and autonomy has brought about a shift from a duty-centered to a rights-centered ethos. As Leo Strauss, renowned political philosopher, put it, "The ego had become the center and origin of the moral world."[4] Whereas previously, rights were derived from duties, duties have now ceased to be primary. Nowadays they arise only as correlatives of the inviolable rights of others which must be respected.

With the enthronement of the human self as the ultimate arbiter of all questions of value, it is hardly surprising that we ultimately arrived at what Christopher Leash, American historian, termed the "age of narcissism." When "doing one's own thing" becomes the overriding norm, all traditional standards of value are eroded. Gone are the days of the Enlightenment, when the vacuum created by the disappearance of traditional authority could be filled by what were perceived as rational duties mandated by the autonomous human conscience.

In the days of Kant, an appeal to reason as the source of ethical values was still feasible. He could claim that autonomous reason was capable of discovering (rather than inventing) universally valid, objective, ethical laws, which are applicable to all rational creatures. But subsequent developments, especially the impact of Marx and Nietzsche on the modern ethos, demolished confidence that reason could provide a secure foundation for morality. As the French philosopher Henri Bergson expressed it, "You can always reason with reason."

The rejection of all external moral authority and the insistence that self-directed autonomy serve as the sole guide for questions of value and morality has culminated in such modern schools of thought as existentialism, ethical emotivism and prescriptivism, which rule out the possibility of maintaining that a particular moral proposition is true.

When ethics are stripped of all objective foundations in either reason or nature, purely arbitrary, subjective decisions remain as the only recourse for ethical decision-making. Small wonder that the resulting moral vacuum has given rise to obsession with self-gratification and has produced an atmosphere of total permissiveness, in which even such a venerable institution as the family has become an endangered species.

Negative freedom

OUR MODERN CONCEPTION OF FREEDOM stresses exclusively the absence of restraints, which Isaiah Berlin, the eminent English philosopher, termed "negative freedom." It is revealing that the inscription on the Liberty Bell "Proclaim liberty to the land and the inhabitants thereof" distorts the Biblical meaning of freedom because it omits the second part of the verse in Leviticus

25:10. What is completely missing is any reference to what the Bible regards as the purpose of liberty, namely, "It shall be a jubilee unto you, and ye shall return every man unto his possession and every man unto his family."[5] As the Bible sees it, human beings must possess roots and links connecting them with their own history, family, and community in order to become truly free.

By now our egocentric morality, which refuses to recognize any form of moral authority, has undermined the foundations of society to such an extent that it has given rise to a worldwide resurgence of crime and violence, endangering the very survival of civilization. It has become increasingly evident that no amount of police can protect a society that has lost its moral moorings.

The difficulties have been exacerbated by the tremendous strides made by modern "value-free" science and technology. One only needs to consider what the computer revolution has wrought in terms of economic dislocation and especially unemployment. In the absence of moral direction, "progress" that could have been an enormous boon to humanity, has become a source of blight and suffering to many. It has given rise to a rapidly growing gap between the "haves" and the "have-nots" – a fault line portending social, economic and political catastrophes.

In reaction to these disturbing developments, a tidal wave of religious fanaticism has been unleashed, which has declared war on the "idols of modernity." Islamic fundamentalism is not alone in demonizing Western democratic values as Satanic. Many religious circles believe that our malaise shows that we are paying dearly for having embraced a value system which extols individuality rather than community and replaces the authority of tradition with that of autonomy.

Religion in the public arena

RELIGION CAN BE STRENGTHENED, rather than weakened, when it resists the temptation to gloat over the bankruptcy of modern secularism. It is my conviction that by integrating our religious values with many of the positive features of modernity, we could simultaneously achieve two objectives. We could revitalize religious faith and at the same time cure many of the sociopathological ailments that plague us.

Some readers may be taken aback by my proposal that religion should enter the public arena and bring to bear its influence for creating a new moral consensus. Nothing is further from my mind than advocating the politicization of religion. But it is imperative that the voice of religiously based *moral* values be heard. One of the worst features of modern secularization was the privatization of religious faith.

To be sure, just as the state must not interfere with the practice of religion, organized religion should refrain from resorting to the political arena to promote a theological agenda. But this does not mean that religion should be relegated to the personal subjective sphere and have no input into the public domain. Even in a pluralistic society, religious individuals have an obligation to express their faith by advocating moral policies, which are inspired by their respective religious beliefs.

Moral opinions do not develop in a vacuum. Inevitably, they are influenced by the world view, be it religious or secular, of the individual holding them. But regardless of their background, they are *moral* intuitions. Hence, there is no reason why, for example, in the abortion debate, religious leaders whose moral positions are obviously related to or grounded in their religious values should not have the same rights as agnostics or atheists in the advocacy of their policies.[6]

It is my belief that at this juncture in history, religion is confronted with the enormous challenge, as well as the extraordinary opportunity, of helping modern man come to grips with the problems arising from a skewed conception of the human self, which by its stress on a one-sided individualism, has resulted in the loss of a sense of community. Having ignored the Biblical dictum that "It is not good for man to be alone," we look upon ourselves as "atomic selves" – as completely detached, unsituated and unencumbered entities – rather than as part of a web of relations.[7]

John Locke, a 17th century British empiricist, erred in depicting the human self as a *tabula rasa* (clean slate), completely free to utilize sense impressions in order to form and combine ideas. It is essential to realize that our way of thinking is not completely molded by our own autonomous selves, but inevitably reflects the impact of the historic communities in which we are situated.

A different understanding of the human self

ONCE WE DISCARD THE NOTION of the unencumbered "atomic self" and replace it with the notion of a "dialogic self," a self which stands in a dialogic relationship with God, we have cleared away the major obstacle blocking our access to transcendence. To utilize such a conception of the self, we need not subscribe to the specific formulation of such modern existentialists as Gabriel Marcel or Martin Buber. Actually, we follow in the footsteps of the position of ancient philosophers such as Plato and Aristotle, who insisted that human beings possess a natural disposition to tend towards the good. Christian religious thinkers, beginning with Augustine through Aquinas to Kierkegaard, have developed this idea into the notion of a natural human aspiration to reach out for God. How deeply ingrained this yearning is, comes to the fore in the writings of an atheistic philosopher such as Sartre, who blames the psychological need for a God for the "bad faith," which manifests itself in many misconceptions about the human condition.

Some modern Jewish thinkers, such as Rav Abraham Isaac Kook and Rav Joseph B. Soloveitchik, also base their approach on the conviction that an analysis of the human psyche points to God. This is why, as we shall note later on, in their analysis of the meaning of *Teshuvah* (repentance), they accept as their basic premise that human beings by nature possess a built-in tendency to strive to come closer to God – the very Source of their being.

A forerunner of the notion of the "dialogic self," may be found in a comment offered in the Palestinian Talmud as an explanation of the Biblical commandment, "Thou shalt not take revenge nor bear grudges against the children of thy people."[8] The prohibition is compared to the proper reaction to a self-inflicted wound. Just as when after inflicting an injury upon oneself, one does not take revenge on the hand that caused the wound, one ought to bear in mind that all of humanity, in a sense, constitutes a single organism, because our fellow human being is actually part of ourselves.[9]

At first blush this statement sounds quite perplexing. Obviously, each organism is only capable of experiencing its own sensations. We may have sympathy with someone else's suffering, but it is impossible to actually feel the pain of another person. Yet one should not dismiss this Talmudic statement as the kind of mysticism expected from adherents of some Eastern mystery cults or from the devotees of "expansion of consciousness," who completely eliminate the distinction between the self and the non-self.

Deeper reflection may reveal that the Sages meant something entirely different. They warned against looking upon the individual self as a totally independent entity, totally unconnected to other selves – the orientation of psychological hedonism which shapes much of modern culture and takes for granted the view that all human motivation is reducible to the quest for individual pleasure.

Even utilitarians, for whom the general welfare of society is the ultimate measure of all morality, seek to buttress their position by appealing to what they believe to be incontrovertible, namely, that all human beings are exclusively motivated by considerations of their own pleasure and pain. Based on this premise, they conclude that the determination of good and evil should be made solely on the basis of the greatest possible balance of pleasure over pain experienced by all members of human society.

Classical Jewish thinkers categorically reject all egocentric approaches because they proceed from the basic premise that, like all of creation, the human self can only be understood when viewed as a creature of God. Such a God-centered perspective extricates us from the narrow confines of a purely egotistical standpoint and enables us to make sense of an organic conception of humanity. Since all human beings bear the image of God, they are equally entitled to reverence for their dignity and to solicitude for their well-being.

By taking seriously our dialogic relationship with God, Who demands compassion and justice towards all creatures bearing His image, we are able to transcend selfishness and thereby advance the unification of humanity. This is why the *Midrash Rabbah* credits Abraham's discovery of monotheism with leading to the process of mending a world that was rent asunder.[10]

The awareness of our rootedness in God Who beckons us to reach out for Him and demands our identification with fellow human beings helps us to overcome our sense of isolation and estrangement from others. This may explain why Leviticus 19:18 adds to the prescription: "Love your fellow humans as yourself" the phrase "I am the Lord." It is on the basis of the growth and expansion of the self through a God-centered perspective that we can feel truly at one with our fellow human beings.

Such self-expansion enhances rather than diminishes the sense of our own worth and dignity. We love ourselves more, rather than less, when we also relate to others with love. We can find true self-fulfillment when we enlarge the range of our concerns and the scope of our activities by encompassing the welfare of our fellow human beings.

Self-love and altruism do not contradict but complement each other. This is why the Torah commands us to love our fellow human beings as we love ourselves. As Rabbi Akiva pointed out, concern for our own lives is not only prescribed, but takes precedence over concern for the lives of others.[11] But if we wish to avoid total spiritual bankruptcy, we must not permit self-love to enjoy a monopoly in our moral economy.

BEYOND AUTONOMY

THE BIBLE TAKES IT FOR GRANTED that the proper functioning of a human self presupposes an appropriate relationship with God and that, therefore, alienation from God engenders self-alienation.

As Kierkegaard, the Christian existentialist, articulated so eloquently, "If he has no God, neither has he a self."[12]

The tragic consequences of an improper relationship with God are pointed out in the Biblical story where Adam and Eve's defiance of God's will resulted in the forfeiture of their idyllic existence in Paradise. Similarly, Cain was condemned to be a "restless wanderer,"[13] because he had committed the sin of fratricide. The prophet Isaiah also graphically depicts the restlessness plaguing sinners:

The wicked are like the troubled sea, for it cannot rest, and its waters cast up mire and dirt, There is no peace for the wicked, saith my God.[14]

The same message is echoed in a comment by the medieval exegete Nachmanides. He notes that the Torah describes Cain as a continuous "builder of cities" rather than, as one would expect, as a man who built cities (in the past). He offers a striking psychological explanation. Because Cain suffered from perpetual restlessness as the consequence of his horrendous crime, he became so dissatisfied with all his accomplishments that immediately after finishing the construction of one city, he was compulsively driven to build another one.[15]

By treating sin as the cause of physical exile and spiritual alienation, the Torah not only connects sin with *Galut* (exile), but conversely links the ingathering of the exiles with Teshuvah.[16] Likewise, Psalm 130 describes the overcoming of alienation and estrangement from God as a process of Redemption. The close connection between sin and exile prompted the Rabbis to arrange the daily *Shemoneh Esreh* in such a manner that the supplication requesting Divine assistance in our efforts to restore our proper relationship with God is immediately followed by a prayer for our Redemption.[17]

The restlessness and turbulence which afflict the sinner also form the background for the prophetic readings which have been selected for Yom Kippur. During the morning service we are exposed to Isaiah's vivid description of the turmoil ravaging the mind and soul of the sinner. This is succinctly summed up in the declaration "there is no peace for the wicked."[18] In the afternoon, we read the tragic story of the prophet Jonah, who becomes a "fugitive from God."[19] Eventually Jonah realizes that any attempt to escape from God is an exercise in futility. This is obviously a fitting message for a day on which we are supposed to stand "before God to become pure."[20] According to Rabbi Akiva, the awareness of our direct and immediate relationship to God provides an antidote to the estrangement from God brought about by our sins. This inspired him to compare the purification attained on Yom Kippur to the cleansing of a ritually impure individual through immersion in a pool of water.[21]

That cultivation of a relationship with God reflects a basic human need is also a cardinal feature of the writings on Repentance by both Rav Abraham Isaac Kook and Rav Joseph B. Soloveitchik. Rav Kook states that "Penitence is inspired by the yearning of all existence to be better, purer, more vigorous and on a higher plane than it is."[22] Similarly, Rav Soloveitchik interprets Teshuvah as the "home-coming" of the soul from the self-imposed exile induced by estrangement from God.[23]

A conception of the self that involves relationship to God is bound to conflict with modern views, which contend that all of ethics revolves around autonomy. We take it for granted that an act or attitude can be moral only if we ourselves recognize it as possessing whatever characteristics we regard as necessary for assigning it the particular status in question. So ingrained is this belief that morality rests upon the authority of the self that we tend to overlook the fact that most of us, when confronted with a moral norm, perceive it not as something invented by ourselves but as something thrust upon us from without.

"It is not good for man to be alone"

THE STARTING POINT OF AUTONOMOUS MORALITY is the human self viewed as a completely detached subject. The etymological meaning of autonomy is self-legislation. It is the *auto* (the self) which is the source of the *nomoi* (the laws). Biblical morality, however, operates with entirely different premises. It takes seriously the implications of Biblical anthropology, which declares that "it is not good for man to be alone."[24] This verse may be interpreted as applying not only to the need for differentiation of the human species into two genders, but also as the characterization of the human condition. We are not self-sufficient entities. Since we cannot function properly in isolation, we must cultivate a sense of community. Many modern thinkers argue that without linkage to a transcendent realm, we cannot achieve proper communion or establish a genuine sense of community.[25]

Our current preoccupation with "doing our own thing" has created a moral vacuum resulting in the utter permissiveness of our society. This clearly shows that, once our connection with transcendence is completely severed, the human self can no longer provide a secure foundation for moral values. Recent developments in ethical theory (e.g., emotivism, prescriptivism) also demonstrate that without a sense of responsibility to an authority other than that of one's own self, we cannot avoid the pitfalls of relativism and subjectivism; we ultimately end up with nihilism.

British philosopher G.E.M. Anscombe has shown in a famous essay that even if moral laws could qualify as dictates of rationality, they still could not command reverence for their authority, unless they were acknowledged as commandments of a

Divine Lawgiver.[26] In her opinion, the Kantian notion of the reverence due to the moral law as such, makes sense only when viewed as the "survival" of a culture which took for granted that moral laws represented the commands of a Divine Lawgiver. For all its flaws, the Kantian "moral argument" for the existence of God shows how deeply Kant's views on morality were rooted in his religious beliefs, which related the moral law to God. It is highly probable that his unwillingness to dispense completely with transcendental sanctions for morality impelled him to accept such doctrines as the existence of God, human freedom, and immortality, as postulates of practical reason.

It may be argued that the ancient Greeks managed to develop an objective ethics without having to invoke a transcendental realm. But it must be borne in mind that theirs was essentially a purely self-serving ethics. For the Greeks ethics was merely a matter of prudence.

Professor Robert Nozick called attention to a crucial difference between Greek and Biblical approaches to ethics. To the Greek mind, ethics represented a branch of knowledge designed to guide individuals in their quest for what constitutes a good life evaluated in terms of self-realization or happiness. The objective of ethics was to instruct individuals in developing their potential for a truly worthwhile existence. Nozick aptly described this as a "push-morality"[27] – a morality designed to enable individuals to overcome obstacles impeding their development into personalities enjoying a happy existence. It was only because humans are social beings that ethics had to include also elements which enable individuals to function properly within society. But it was the concern for the well-being of the individual, not for that of society as a whole, which provided the foundation of this ethics.

Although Greek ethics included elements designed to instruct individuals in functioning properly within society, this was due to the fact that humans are by nature *social* beings and could not attain happiness, unless they played a role within society. But it was out of concern for the personal well-being of the individual, not for that of society as a whole, that ethical rules were prescribed for individuals.

As against the self-centeredness of Greek morality, Biblical morality consists not of counsels spelling out what was needed to satisfy the self's requirements for well-being, but of demands addressed *to* the self. The prophet asks, "What does God demand of thee?"[28] The Bible, to employ Nozick's terminology, operates with a "pull-morality," because the self is pulled by the claims of the other. As I argued in my *Ethics of Responsibility*,[29] in the Jewish view, we are supposed to *respond* to God's claims upon us. Modern Jewish thinkers such as Martin Buber, Franz Rosenzweig, Emmanuel Levinas and Rav Joseph B. Soloveitchik, despite all their profound differences, agree that Judaism grounds all ethics in demands addressed to us by God rather than by society or the self.

In this context it hardly matters whether we treat these heteronomous ethical demands as communicated to us by revelation, reason, sentiment, or conscience. What is important is that they are apprehended as demands emanating from a transcendent realm. Otherwise it would be difficult to explain why ethical values are perceived to be endowed with unconditional and absolute authority (trumping all other values and overriding all intellectual, aesthetic or pragmatic considerations).

This is why Jews could not subscribe to the Greek motto "Know thyself" as the epitome of all wisdom. Instead, they adopted the formulation of the Psalmist, "I am constantly aware of the Presence of God"[30] and looked upon "the fear of God as the beginning of all wisdom."[31] Maimonides went so far as to look upon the "knowledge of God" as the very purpose of all human existence.[32]

Significance of charity

A TELLING ILLUSTRATION of the egocentricity of Greek ethics is furnished by its attitude to charity. Since friends are indispensable to a worthwhile life, one must show solicitude for their well-being and assist them in their hour of need. But no such concern is mandated for strangers. In the Jewish scheme, however, charity is not based upon the pursuit of self-interest. All the destitute, weak and oppressed are entitled to our assistance. We are told to "Love your neighbor as yourself," not out of egotistical considerations, but because, as the sequel of the verse states,

"I am the Lord your God."[33]

Secular ethics, which rejects any kind of theological prop for ethics, finds it extremely difficult to provide a foundation for its value-system. The roots of the problem can be traced back to the atomistic conception of the self, which originated with the French philosopher, Descartes, and treats the self as a totally independent subject. Unless we discard this conception and return to that of the "dialogic self," we find ourselves in the condition brought about by Humpty Dumpty's fall. All our attempts to put together the insulated self with transcendence cannot succeed. A Chassidic teacher once captured this insight with a far-fetched interpretation of a Biblical verse. It was poor exegesis, but it conveyed a profound truth. Commenting on the passage (Deut. 5:4) "I stand between God and you," he noted that it is the undue emphasis upon the human ego that erects a barrier between man and God.

The existence of God

WHAT EXACERBATES THE MODERN value-crisis is another component of the modern ethos which also can be traced back to Descartes. Prior to this revolutionary thinker, nature was conceived as being replete with purposes and values. In the ancient world, nature was viewed as teleological, as exhibiting purposes and goals. Hence, nature could serve as the source of guidance on how best to realize the values and ends which would satisfy the requirements of human nature. But Descartes' insistence upon exclusively mechanistic explanations delegitimized all "final causes." Facts and values became completely separate. It was, therefore, no longer possible to invoke the authority of nature for ethical guidance. This, in turn, led to a situation where, in the absence of transcendental props, ethics became a matter of purely subjective, intuitive beliefs, that basically amounted merely to matters of personal preference or taste.

The notion that a transcendental authority is a prerequisite for morality, however, does not in itself prove that such a source of authority is available. As we noted previously, the existence of a need does not warrant the inference that there exists anyone or anything capable of satisfying such a need. Not every question has an answer and not every problem has a solution.

It must, however, be borne in mind that religious faith is by no means the only approach to reality which defies purely rational explanation and justification. For all its usefulness in predicting future phenomena and as an effective means of controlling the forces of nature, science can hardly qualify as a satisfactory *explanation* of the world we encounter. It merely renders an account of the "what" of the laws of nature, but does not seek an answer to the question of why the laws of nature are what they are. Moreover, science can provide a useful method for describing the phenomena of our experience only on the basis of a host of presuppositions (such as the uniformity of nature, the existence of an objective world) the validity of which cannot be demonstrated.

Since even the validity of science cannot be demonstrated, I am not uncomfortable with the fact that most thinkers agree that there is no proof for the existence of God. Even Kant, who viewed the moral "proof" for the existence of God as a postulate of practical reason, declared that it was necessary to demolish the theoretical arguments for the existence of God in order to make room for faith. There is a limit to what can be rationally demonstrated. In the final analysis, all depends upon our choice of categories which we employ for the interpretation of our experience of the world. Asked "Where God could be found," Rav Menachem Mendel of Kotzk replied, "Wherever He is admitted."

There is no irrefutable evidence of the existence of God which could convince radical empiricists, who *a priori* rule out the possibility of supernatural intervention. Even if it were possible to produce video tapes of the Sinaitic Revelation, they would still say "let us find the natural causes of this extraordinary and puzzling event." Any recourse to supernatural causes would be categorically rejected by them.[34]

It is entirely our choice whether we want to explain the world purely in naturalistic categories and therefore treat religious faith as a phenomenon to be explained *away* (courtesy of Freud or Durkheim) or whether we wish to adopt a conceptual scheme, which, in addition to naturalistic modes of explanation, also is prepared to acknowledge a transcendental realm, which can be invoked for ethical and spiritual purposes. We have to realize that were we to insist on a exclusively naturalistic vocabulary, we would be utterly bereft of any guidance in the area that matters most, namely, our conduct.

This is an existential choice we cannot abdicate to any one else. My avenue to faith is the reverse of reason seeking faith. It is my existential choice of faith that prompts me to search for rational support for my religious beliefs. In the final analysis, cognitive factors cannot resolve the question whether to accept or reject religious faith; it is a purely subjective decision, responsibility for which is one of the burdens imposed upon us by human freedom. We cannot escape responsibility for choosing the categories with which we seek to understand our world. It is up to us whether to rely solely upon purely naturalistic categories, which leave no room for the supernatural, or whether we are prepared to explain our experiences in terms that do not rule out the incursion of the supernatural upon our world.[35]

THE SEARCH FOR MEANING AND PURPOSE

AMONG THE STRONGEST ATTRACTIONS of a theistic world view is its ability to provide a sense of meaning and purpose for our existence. A purely scientific approach is incapable of satisfying this basic human need.

As we noted in the previous chapter, ever since Descartes' rejection of final causes left mechanistic causation as the exclusive explanation of all natural phenomena, it was impossible for those who follow his approach to find any sense of meaning in the universe. Small wonder, then, that so many philosophers echo Sartre's contention that any claim that human existence has meaning represents merely an act of "bad faith" or self-deception.

It is, however, very difficult for many individuals to reconcile themselves to such a dismal point of view. After all, William James already recognized that the need to be needed is one of the most essential requirements for mental health. We cannot function properly without the conviction that we serve a purpose in the world.

Religious faith as the source of meaning and purpose

IT IS THIS NEED WHICH RELIGIOUS FAITH is eminently qualified to satisfy. A theistic perspective assures us that we are creatures, not of blind chance, but of an omnipotent and benevolent God, Who has assigned us a role in His Providential design.

Thus religious faith, assuring us that events are governed by Divine Providence, dispenses with the need to find explanations for events that in the absence of such a faith would strike us as absurd.[36] The religious believer, however, looks upon the universe not as a self-sufficient cosmos, but as the creation of a transcendent God, the source of all existence, value and meaning. It is, therefore, no longer necessary to answer questions concerning the meaning of any event in terms of immanent purposes manifesting themselves in nature or history. Natural events at the very most can disclose only fragmentary meanings. This is dramatically illustrated in the Book of Job, when questions about Divine justice are disposed of by showing that the human mind cannot fathom the purposes of a transcendent, infinite God.

The affirmation of the Jewish liturgy that "God created everything for His glory,"[37] does not really provide any form of teleological explanation. It does not shed any light on why a particular entity possesses the specific set of characteristics with which it is endowed. We have no way of knowing why a different set of properties would not have served equally well to glorify God. According to Maimonides, the affirmation merely states that we are unable to comprehend the purpose of any creature and that, therefore, we cannot go beyond the assertion that any given creature exists, because God has willed its existence.[38]

Obviously, such an approach cannot be utilized to explain the purpose served by any *particular* event or existence. No matter what happens, the religious believer will maintain that the occurrence of every conceivable event serves an inexplicable Divine purpose. But since the non-occurrence of a given event or the absence of a particular characteristic in question would also be explained in exactly the same fashion, we cannot claim that the proposition "whatever exists, exists for the sake of God," has explanatory value; for what explains everything, really explains nothing.[39]

Although both believers and existentialist atheists alike are incapable of discovering a meaningful structure within the universe, a fundamental difference between the two must be noted. Whereas atheistic existentialists are situated within a world of absurdity in which all meaning and purpose amount merely to wishful fabrications or projections of individuals, believers find themselves in a universe that reflects the inexplicable purpose and providential plan of a benevolent God.

It is only because of the limitations of our human perspective that we can speak of the absurdities of existence. How could reality be absurd if it represents a Divine creation, governed by His Providence? As Saadiah Gaon noted,[40] the Biblical account of creation, with God pronouncing the verdict "it was very good" after the completion of the process, cannot be reconciled with a pessimism that reduces all existence to total meaninglessness and purposelessness.

The optimism engendered by the belief that the world is the creation of a benevolent God, Who has a specific purpose for every creature, is not diminished by the consciousness of the intrinsic limitations arising from our finitude.

Unlike other-worldly religions, Judaism is life-affirming. It does not seek to provide an escape mechanism from the imperfections of our material world, but stresses this worldly human responsibilities. "One hour devoted to the Torah and good deeds in this world is superior to all the life in the hereafter."[41]

Our religious ideal is not the enjoyment of eternal bliss but the fulfillment of God's will in this world of finite existence. We celebrate life in the here and now, because this is where we can fulfill our mission. We are not mystics who yearn for the dissolution of their individuality through mystic union with God. Our highest goal is communion, not union, with Him. Were man to lose his individuality completely in God, he would no longer be able to remain in a covenantal relationship with Him.

As Martin Buber emphasized, the very possibility of such a relationship presupposes that human beings do not merge with God but enter into a dialogic relationship with Him, by responding to His love and committing themselves to His service.

Since the task assigned to humans can only be carried out by finite creatures composed of both matter and spirit, a religious perspective enables us to welcome our finitude as indispensable to our ability to execute our unique mission to become God's partners in the creation of the world. It is this mission which endows our finite efforts with the potential for infinite significance. This is why, before studying Torah, Jews recite a blessing praising God for "having given us a Torah of truth and implanting within us a life of eternity."

The Kaddish

A TELLING ILLUSTRATION OF THE JEWISH ATTITUDE towards the transcendent meaning of our finite life is found in the Kaddish prayer which mourners recite as they confront the mystery of human existence. The Kaddish contains no reference whatsoever to the phenomenon of death, but it indirectly conveys the Jewish response to the finitude of our existence. When human life is evaluated within the larger context of the ultimate objective of Judaism – the sanctification of the Divine Name – confrontation with the tragic finality of death will no longer result in a declaration of futility. Instead, life will be endowed with meaning to the extent that it contributes to the realization of the Providential design by helping to bring the world closer to the Messianic Redemption.

Freedom and responsibility

JUDAISM EMPHASIZES THAT HUMAN BEINGS radically differ from all other organic or inorganic beings. They are the only creatures who are not completely subject to the operation of the determinism of causal law, but are endowed with freedom of the will. All other creatures automatically fulfill their purpose, because they have no choice but to conform to God's will. Human beings, however, as bearers of the image of God, are not just helpless puppets in the hands of an omnipotent deity. They have the ability to either glorify or profane God, because, for all His omnipotence, He, for mysterious reasons, has willed that human beings, through their freely rendered service, may become partners with Him in the process of creation.

The most important area for the exercise of human freedom and creativity is that of the human self. The Bible describes the creation of human beings in terms completely different from those of other creatures. As a rule, the creation of the various natural phenomena is introduced by the phrase "Let there be."[42] But in describing the creation of man, the Book of Genesis refrains from employing this expression and replaces it with "Let us make."[43] The emphasis upon *making* in the creation of human beings indicates that, unlike other creatures, man is not a finished product but is forever in the making. Thus, in the Biblical view, humans have no fixed, predetermined nature. We are what we make of ourselves. As the existentialist philosopher, Karl Jaspers, put it, "To be a man is to *become* a man."

The notion of human responsibility presupposes that human beings are not completely dominated by psychological determinism but can exercise a measure of control over their development. Although Teshuvah is frequently mistranslated as repentance, its real meaning is returning, [to what we would have become, had we not deviated from the proper path]. Essentially, Teshuvah amounts to self-creation. As long as a human being is alive, s/he has the potential to acquire a new identity.

Creativity

RABBI JOSEPH B. SOLOVEITCHIK TIME AND AGAIN pointed to the centrality of creativity in Judaism.[44] He contended that the Torah does not begin with the account of creation in Genesis in order to impart cosmological or metaphysical knowledge. The real objective of the narrative is a normative one, to teach us how to conduct our lives. Since the Biblical command "thou shalt walk in His ways"[45] mandates that human beings emulate God, they must strive to imitate the Creator's creativity. Hence, to become creative in the effort to help perfect the world emerges as a religio-ethical ideal.[46]

Human partnership with God involves not only our responsibility to advance civilization but also to participate in determining the meaning of the Written Torah. We depend upon the Oral Torah in order to ascertain the meaning of the written word. To cite just one example, the Talmud provides compelling logical reasons why the Torah's formulation "eye for eye, tooth for tooth, hand for hand, foot for foot"[47] must not be taken literally, but should be interpreted as referring to monetary compensation.[48] Thus, the Oral Torah assigns to human reason and conscience a decisive role in ascertaining the meaning of the revealed word of God as contained in the Written Torah. This being the case, the meaning of the Torah is the product of the interaction between the infinite God and finite man.

The Talmud maintains that a special covenant has been established between God and Israel charging Israel with the task of developing the Oral Torah.[49] Thus, the very conception of an Oral Torah involves, in addition to unconditional surrender to the authority of revealed teachings, creative efforts on the part of human beings, who employ their intelligence and moral insights in the quest for shaping a "Torah of life."

The emphasis upon human creativity also manifests itself in the categorical rejection of all supernatural influences on the determination of the meaning of the Torah. In the quest to understand the Torah we are supposed to rely exclusively on our own rational resources and ethical intuitions. According to the Talmud, "We do not pay attention to heavenly voices ...[for] the Torah is not in heaven."[50] Maimonides even brands as a "false prophet" whoever offers legal opinions not on the basis of rational arguments but by claiming support of a supernatural revelation for his position.[51] A prophet is authorized to appeal to supernatural instructions only for meeting the exigencies of the moment (including even the temporary suspension of Torah Law). Prophecy, however, may not be utilized for the clarification of legal matters. Were prophets granted any special authority to utilize their supernatural powers for the determination of legal issues, Torah would cease to be the joint product of the partnership between God and man.

In Jewish mystical thought the notion of this partnership is expanded considerably. The Zohar's central doctrine that "the stirring below must precede the stirring on high" makes God in some sense dependent on human beings. Human initiative is needed to start a cosmic chain reaction whose repercussions reverberate in the highest regions of being. The process of *Tikkun*, involving the redemption of the universe from evil and the ultimate re-unification of God with His *Shekhinah* must originate with human creative efforts. In his well-known classic, *God in Search of Man*, Abraham J. Heschel eloquently reformulated these mystical doctrines for the modern reader.

The anthropocentric orientation of the Kabbalah by no means represents a break with the Rabbinic tradition. The Talmud already contains statements to the effect that God, whose Shekhinah is in exile, is also redeemed together with the redemption of the world. Thus we are told that "wherever they [the people of Israel] went into exile, the Shekhinah went with them."[52] Similarly, the Talmud interprets Isaiah 63:9 as meaning "In all their affliction He [God] was afflicted."[53]

Such an anthropocentric orientation clearly refutes the claim of some materialists and existentialists that religion's emphasis upon Divine power and goodness devalues human beings. On the contrary, it clearly shows that Jewish faith confers infinite value and significance upon human existence and elevates rather than lowers the status of humanity.

GOD-CENTEREDNESS VERSUS SELF-CENTEREDNESS

AS WE PREVIOUSLY EMPHASIZED, the expectation that religious faith will enhance our existence cannot serve as justification for theistic belief. The benefits derived from embracing a religious faith must be regarded as welcome by-products, not as the ground for our belief in monotheism. A religion based not upon sincere conviction but upon wishful thinking deserves to be dismissed as an "opiate of the people."

Although Judaism treats belief in Divine reward and punishment as an article of faith, it focuses upon obedience to Divine commandments rather than upon salvation. The Talmud points out that although Abraham was by no means the first monotheist, he pioneered the conception of God as the "Master"[54] to be served rather than the supreme Power upon Whose assistance we depend for the satisfaction of our needs or desires.

In pagan cults, the purpose of worship was not the service of the deity. Instead, sacrifices and rites were offered in the hope that the performance of various cultic rites would succeed in manipulating the gods to do our bidding. Worship was viewed as a *quid pro quo*. In exchange for the gifts offered to them, the gods were expected to reciprocate favorably.

In striking contrast with this orientation, for Judaism the service of God is not a means but constitutes in itself the highest ideal. Thus the basic difference between monotheism and polytheism is not just the number of deities acknowledged. It rather reflects an altogether different approach to the very nature and function of religious commitment. As a well-known saying of the Talmud admonishes us, "Be not like slaves who serve their master in order to receive compensation."[55] Maimonides goes so far as to contend that the ideal of serving God out of love can be attained only when consideration of rewards (including the expectation of bliss in the hereafter) ceases to be a factor and when we are motivated solely by the desire to serve God.[56]

Characteristic of the Jewish approach to religion is the fact that whenever we read a text in which the Tetragrammaton (the proper name for God) occurs, we do not pronounce it as written but as *A-donai* (my Master). But why was this particular appellation chosen? Since there is no connection whatsoever between the letters forming the Tetragrammaton and the accepted pronunciation, there are numerous terms that could have been selected. One might have referred to the deity as E-lohim (God of Power or Justice), as *Shaddai* (the Almighty) or as *Avinu Shebashamayim* (our Father in Heaven). Why then was the name A-donai preferred?

A simple answer suggests itself. What matters from a Jewish perspective above all is that we relate to God as the Supreme Master, to Whom we belong and Whose commands we obey because He is our Sovereign.

The Shema

SIGNIFICANTLY, THE TALMUD REFERS to the daily recital of the Shema as the "acceptance of the yoke of the kingdom of Heaven."[57] The choice of terminology, which describes the basic tenets of our monotheism as submission to a yoke, illustrates that Judaism looks upon religion primarily as a form of service to God rather than as an instrumentality designed to secure personal benefits.

The belief in the Oneness of God represents not merely a fundamental metaphysical truth; it also holds enormous normative implications. The Torah text itself links the affirmation of

His Oneness with the commandment, "Love the Lord, thy God, with all thy heart, with all thy soul, and with all thy might."[58] This is a perfectly logical connection. If we are to take the Oneness of God seriously, He alone really matters and all our concerns must revolve exclusively around Him. As Rabbi Akiva explained when asked why he could be so cheerful while dying a martyr's death and suffering excruciating pain from his Roman tormentors:

> *Throughout my life, whenever I recited the Shema and reached the verse, "Thou shalt love the Lord, thy God, with all thy soul," which means even at the cost of your life, I wondered when I would be given the opportunity to fulfill this commandment. Now that I have it, should I not fulfill it.*[59]

Based upon this precedent, some Rabbinic authorities recommend that during the recital of the Shema we should resolve to give up our lives and die a martyr's death – if necessary – to demonstrate our total commitment to God in this fashion.

But this unconditional surrender is not only required in extreme situations. Because human beings bear the image of God and are mandated to walk in His ways, the commandment to engage in *Yichud Ha-Shem* (the affirmation of the oneness, unity and uniqueness of God) engenders another task. We are mandated to emulate God by striving to unify ourselves. All our diverse faculties should be devoted to the pursuit of one all-inclusive goal – the service of God. In the words of the prayer uttered before the recital of the Shema, "Unify our hearts to love and fear Thy Name."[60] Obviously, love and fear are totally different emotions. But both are necessary ingredients of a truly worthwhile human existence and should be harnessed in the service of God.

With its theocentrism, the Shema represents the classic challenge to overcome the human tendency towards egocentricity, which Walt Whitman so aptly dubbed, "egotheism." We are challenged to replace our preoccupation with self-gratification and self-fulfillment with a life style in which all activities and interests focus exclusively upon the service of God.

God-Centeredness Versus Self-Centeredness

The emphasis upon our total subordination to the sovereignty of God also explains why during the recital of the Shema we find it necessary to interrupt the reading of the biblical text in order to insert the phrase, "Blessed be the name of the glory of His Kingdom forever." Apparently, the Jewish tradition wanted to make sure that the affirmation of the theological tenets of monotheism explicitly include a reference to God's sovereignty. The importance attached to the proclamation of His sovereignty also comes to the fore in the Jewish law which stipulates that without a reference to God as "King of the universe," no prayer can be accorded the status of a *Berakhah* (Benediction).[61]

According to Rashi, the author of the most popular traditional commentary on the Torah, the Shema also contains a reference to the belief that the sovereignty of God sooner or later will be universally recognized. Accordingly, "Hear, Oh Israel, the Lord our God is One" should be interpreted "the Lord, who [presently] is acknowledged only as our God, will [eventually] be acknowledged by all of humanity as the one and only God."[62] The attainment of this ultimate goal is reserved for the Messianic Redemption. In the words of the prophet Zechariah, "On that day God will be the King of the entire earth."[63]

Similarly, the prophet Isaiah focuses upon the universal acknowledgment of God's sovereignty in his portrayal of the Messianic Redemption. "They shall not hurt nor destroy in all My holy Mountain; for the earth shall be full of the knowledge of the Lord, as the waters cover the sea."[64] The abolition of war, violence and oppression and the emergence of a moral world of justice, peace and universal respect for human dignity are viewed as by-products of humanity's acknowledgment of the sovereignty of God.

A slave of God

IN KEEPING WITH THE EMPHASIS upon the absolute rule of God, total commitment to His service represents the acme of religious perfection. There are no limits to this God-centered approach. The scope of piety transcends conformity to explicit instructions or obedience to specific norms. There are no religiously neutral zones. Depending upon our motivation, every act can acquire religious significance.

As the Talmud[65] puts it, the verse "in all your ways, you shall know Him"[66] describes the range of activities over which the religious ideal holds sway. According to Maimonides, however intrinsically worthwhile an objective may be, like preservation of our health, ideally it should be treated as a means towards the service of God.[67] This is in keeping with Hillel's maxim, "Let all your actions be for the sake of God." [68]

Because of the all-absorbing and all-demanding nature of religious commitment, the highest accolade that Judaism can bestow upon any person is to be a "slave of God." Moses earned this honorific term, because he had absolutely no selfish agenda. No matter how high the cost to him personally, he devoted his life to the service of God and never wavered in his commitment to carry out the mission which God had assigned to him.

To be a slave of God, Rabbi Joseph B. Soloveitchik emphasized, involves more than merely being His servant. Servants retain their independent status. They have only specific duties and limited responsibilities. Slaves, on the other hand, have no rights vis a vis their owners, because they are deemed the property of the latter. Jewish law operates on the principle that whatever a slave acquires automatically belongs to the owner.[69] Hence the ideal of being a slave of God calls for the freely given commitment on the part of an individual to forego all other objectives and to focus exclusively upon the fulfillment of the will of God.

An ancient Rabbinic commentary, the Mekhilta, develops this notion in conjunction with the exposition of the first commandment of the Decalogue. "I am the Lord, thy God, Who took thee out of the land of Egypt, the house of bondage."[70]

We are reminded that our status was changed from that of slaves of Pharaoh to slaves of God. But this form of enslavement actually represents a form of liberation and a guarantee of human dignity, for after all we "are slaves of God, not slaves of other slaves."[71]

Surrender to God as a source of freedom

FAR FROM LOOKING UPON THIS total commitment to God as a form of self-denial or self-alienation, Judaism views it as a source of freedom. According to an often-cited Rabbinic comment, "only those who occupy themselves with Torah, can be called truly free."[72]

Without Torah, we are enslaved by our appetites and passions. It is only by leading a God-centered life that we extricate ourselves from various forms of idolatry, including that of self-deification, and become truly free to fulfill the mission, which God, the source of all value and existence, has assigned to us. It is against this background that we can understand why the prayerbook declares that Torah "is our life."

The dialectical relationship between total surrender to God and the achievement of genuine freedom is expressed in a Talmudic comment on the first chapter of Psalms.[73] The biblical text states that "Happy is the man whose delight is in the Torah of the Lord and in His Torah doth he meditate by day and night."[74]

The Rabbis, however, make use of the ambiguity of the Hebrew text. The word *uvetorato* can be interpreted as referring to God's Torah or to man's Torah. They suggest the second interpretation and contend that at the beginning it is "the Torah of the Lord" – but after an individual immerses himself in the Torah, it becomes *his* very own, no longer merely His Torah.

When Torah is internalized, it no longer represents a heteronomous law, it but reflects the dictates of the autonomous self. This is, perhaps, what Menachem Mendel of Kotzk had in mind when, pleading for total identification with God's will, he ingeniously rendered the verse (Psalm 81:10) "Let there not be within you a strange God" as "Let God not be a stranger within you."

When we reach the stage of becoming so attached to God that we will do only what He wills, we have attained the ideal of *Deveikut,* clinging to God. In the opinion of many Jewish thinkers, this is the most intimate relationship that finite human beings can attain with an infinite God.

THE ROLE OF ARGUMENTS FOR THE EXISTENCE OF GOD

WE CONCLUDED THE LAST CHAPTER by stating that Deveikut is the acme of religious perfection. This kind of attachment to God represents the very antithesis of self-centeredness or self-sufficiency.

As noted in the last chapter, in sharp contrast to Feuerbach, whose views prepared the ground for Marxism, our tradition views God-centeredness not as a source of self-alienation but of self-fulfillment. This, in turn, reflects the Jewish view that the human self is not a self-enclosed substance but stands in dialogic relationship with God.

Deveikut

SIGNIFICANTLY, THE TERM *DAVAK* (TO CLING) is first found in the Torah (Genesis 2:25) with reference to the relationship of intimacy that should be attained by spouses before becoming one flesh.[75] According to the Biblical account, God took a rib (according to other interpretations, a side) from Adam out of which Eve was formed. This inspired the Midrash to declare that a male is incomplete until he recovers the lost dimension of his existence through marriage to a woman, when two distinct selves are re-united and joined into a larger one.[76]

In Deuteronomy 11:23 and 30:20 the same expression, davak, is used to describe the ultimate religious goal – the attainment of Deveikut with God. To be sure, Judaism objects to the notion that human beings can actually merge with God, but with respect to our relation with the deity, Deveikut means that we become so attached to Him that we overcome our existential loneliness by completely identifying with His purposes and goals. In the words of the Talmud, "Treat His will as if it were your own will."[77]

Because of its aversion to dichotomies between the physical and the spiritual, the Bible does not hesitate to employs identical terms for the description of the relationship between spouses and the highest degree of attachment to God. Similarly, the *Song of Songs* was admitted into the Holy Writ because its erotic images were interpreted by the Sages as metaphors for the love of God. In keeping with this precedent, Maimonides unabashedly advocates that we cultivate the love of God to such a degree that its intensity will surpass the passion drawing human lovers to each other.[78]

Conscience and Teshuvah

THE CONCEPTION OF A HUMAN SELF in dialogue with God radically clashes with views which treat the human conscience merely as the voice of our own selves. While Freud regarded conscience as the internalization of norms emanating from authority figures and Martin Heidegger defined conscience as the call of the authentic self to a self which has lost itself in the everyday world, Judaism maintains that conscience is grounded in our relationship with God. It is interesting that, according to Maimonides, confession of sins is not merely an act of introspection, but also involves the consciousness that we are in communion with God.[79]

The well-known verse, "Come now and let us reason together, saith the Lord, though your sins prove to be like scarlet, they shall become white as snow"[80] is actually a mistranslation.

A more accurate translation would replace "let us reason together," with "let us face up to each other." According to the prophet, what is required for spiritual regeneration is not merely a sound reasoning process, but the awareness of our dialogic relationship with God.

The real objective of such activities as repentance and confession, which form an integral part of the Teshuvah process, is not so much seeking atonement for our sins or winning forgiveness as it is to bring about the creation of a new self. The objective is succinctly described by the Psalmist in the words, "A pure heart, oh God, create for me, and a steadfast spirit renew within me."[81] The goal to be reached – the emergence of a new personality – presupposes breaking the chains of causality that operate in psychological determinism.

The Jewish ideal of Teshuvah, therefore, involves an act of *self-creation* in the fullest sense of the term. The change of direction brought about by Teshuvah cannot be attributed to antecedent psychological causes but represents the triumph of the free, creative spirit over the realm of nature which is governed by the rule of the causal law. It is through the return of the self to its proper relation with the very source of its being – the acknowledgment of the dialogic nature of the self – that a person's personality is radically transformed.

When a human self is completely self-enclosed and totally preoccupied with its own gratification through either higher or lower pleasures, it is so crippled that it can hardly focus on any other value. At the very best, considerations of justice, decency or integrity can play a role only as purely instrumental values designed to promote the self-interest of the agent. It is through openness to transcendence that we can best extricate ourselves from egocentricity and make room for various values which are not directly related to the well-being of the agent.

This may well be the reason why the Sages contended that "we become free only through engagement with Torah."[82] Paradoxical though it may sound, the ideal of self-liberation calls for casting off the shackles of "self-service," which hold in bondage all those whose lives are immersed in the quest for self-gratification, self-fulfillment or self-realization. In his *Tanya*, Rav Shneur Zalman of Liadi observed that we are mandated to make reference to the Exodus from Egypt when we recite the Shema (the acknowledgment of the yoke of Heaven) in order that we may become aware that true self-liberation necessitates total commitment to the service of God[83]

It is highly likely that the Biblical expression of "circumcising the foreskin of our hearts"[84] corresponds to what we would call cultivating "openness to transcendence." Similarly, many prayers plead for the "opening of our hearts through Torah." Implicit in this conception is the belief that it is only failure to remove obstacles blocking a healthy relationship with God which prevent us from perceiving the dialogic nature of the human self.

No need for proofs

IT IS IN THIS LIGHT THAT WE CAN APPRECIATE why the Bible is so indifferent to proofs of the existence of God and confines itself to pointing to historical experiences which provided the opportunity to encounter God. To the true believer, nothing is more certain than the existence of God. As Kierkegaard put it, a lover does not question the existence of his beloved. When the human self stands in dialogical relationship to God, it does not seek proofs for His existence.

In the modern world we are not surprised that most people totally ignore epistemological questions such as the reliability of sense perception or the validity of induction, but simply take for granted the common sense view that there is an external world subject to the causal law. Similarly, in antiquity the experience of the sense of dependence upon supernatural powers was regarded as adequate ground for belief in the existence of a supernatural realm. This is why even the Epicureans did not question the existence of gods. They never challenged the basic premises of polytheistic paganism. They merely claimed that the gods were totally detached from human affairs.

The Bible, therefore, does not find it necessary to argue against a totally secularized conception of the world. Instead, it had to guard against the human tendency to idolize various forces and powers. The absolutization of any power, value or agent other than God constitutes idolatry, which in Rabbinic terminology is branded as "sacrifices to the dead,"[85] – a life-negating form of spiritual death.

In the modern era we have reached a level of sophistication and skepticism where the belief in the existence of a Supernatural Being is no longer generally held. There is simply no way in which the traditional arguments for the existence of God, be they cosmological, ontological or moral, can be revived to convince the non-believer that belief in God is a valid inference from other rational beliefs.

Before Kant wrought his "Copernican revolution" in philosophy, many rationalists subscribed to Aquinas' basic tenets that without a belief in the existence of God it was not possible to provide an intelligible account of either nature or morality. But the emergence of critical philosophy underscored the limitations of the human mind and dismissed all metaphysical explanations as sheer conjecture. Although most empiricists reject the positivistic claim that metaphysical statements are totally meaningless, it is widely agreed that neither atheism nor theism can be treated as analogous to scientific hypotheses.[86]

Natural theology versus supernatural theology

THE INTELLECTUAL CURRENTS PREVAILING nowadays cannot be reconciled with the basic tenet of natural theology, which states that we can draw objectively valid inferences from the world to the existence and attributes of God. Kant has succeeded in discrediting the rationalistic tradition, which claimed that the existence of God was a hypothesis necessary to render an intelligible account of the universe.

Nowadays most scientists, believers or atheists alike, will agree that metaphysical questions such as the existence of God cannot be settled by recourse to scientific methods. They will sympathize with the position of LaPlace in his famous exchange with Napoleon. After hearing a brief explanation of the Kant-Laplace theory of the origin of the universe, the French emperor asked: "But according to your theory, which states that the universe evolved from the rotation of gases, what was God's role in the formation of the universe"? Whereupon LaPlace replied, "I do not need this hypothesis."

Since it is generally accepted that theistic belief cannot be grounded in purely objective considerations, religious faith, in the final analysis, becomes a matter of existential choice. In the absence of incontrovertible evidence for either theism or atheism, it is up to us to decide whether or not we wish to rule out *a priori* the very possibility of any kind of supernatural intervention in the world.

By ruling out the incursion of the supernatural, we commit ourselves to describing the world exclusively in purely naturalistic categories and limiting ourselves to scientific methods and procedures in accounting for the various phenomena we experience. Exclusive reliance on scientific explanation leaves us no choice but to admit that all we can expect to achieve is to predict the occurrence of other phenomena. We must, however, give up any hope to *understand* the whys and wherefores of the world. Religious faith, on the other hand, will provide supernatural explanations for the very existence of a universe. This being the case, we may prefer to accept the possibility that some of our experiences are caused by supernatural factors. We, therefore, may prefer to adopt a set of categories which are compatible with the requirements of religious faith.

Science itself is completely neutral on this issue. "Scientism," the belief that there can be no supernatural interventions, must be categorically rejected since it is not a scientific theory but a dogma which cannot be supported by scientific evidence. It is one thing to contend that scientific methodology rules out recourse to supernatural intervention or explanation, and another to maintain that there are no supernatural causes. Thus scientism, no less than the belief in a Creator, rests on an act of faith. Moreover, the soundness of scientific methodology has never been demonstrated. It, too, presupposes a variety of assumptions (e.g., the validity of the principle of induction). Significantly, a major work by George Santayana is entitled *Science and Animal Faith*. As the title suggests, the entire scientific enterprise presupposes *faith* in the existence of an external world governed by laws which are obtained by inductive inferences. Or as Professor Quine put it, science is one of many languages that could be employed to describe our experiences. Although the validity of science cannot be demonstrated, we utilize the language of science, because it has been found to be an extremely valuable language to describe our experience of the world. But this does not deny the possibility that some other languages may be more appropriate for aesthetic, ethical or religious purposes.

The issue between believers and non-believers boils down to the choice of categories. It resembles debates between competing schools of philosophy, which are generally recognized to be exercises in futility, because they do not understand each other. They degenerate into monologues. Dialogues are possible only when there is a common universe of discourse. In the absence of a shared language we find ourselves in the position of the builders of the tower of Babel, whose design was thwarted when their languages were confounded so that no one could understand what a fellow human being had to say.

It should, therefore, not be surprising that the acceptance of a theistic belief system must rest upon our own decision whether to chose a set of categories by which the religious experience (like Schleiermacher's feeling of absolute dependence) may be explained or whether it should be explained away as mere self-delusion. It is left entirely to our choice whether to insist dogmatically upon a purely naturalistic approach to reality or whether we are prepared to allow the possibility of the intrusion of the Supernatural intrusion upon the realm of the natural.[87]

Documentary hypothesis

SOME BIBLE CRITICS CLAIM that in the light of modern scholarship we can no longer cling to the belief that the Bible is a Divinely revealed document. Actually, this view is far from being of modern vintage. It originated with Spinoza who, as a radical rationalist, felt constrained to rule out the possibility of any supernatural communication or intervention.

Walter Kaufmann, a prominent agnostic modern philosopher, pointed out that rejection of the traditional view of the Bible as the word of God was not due to the "discoveries" of modern Biblical scholarship.[88] Such a claim would be putting the cart before the horse. On the contrary, it was largely due to the combined influence of Hegel's philosophy of history and Darwin's theory of evolution. The belief that the evolution of the historic process constituted the progressive revelation of the Absolute (God) provided the inspiration for the critical method, which aimed to interpret Scripture simply as a purely human document and not as the record of a supernatural Divine Revelation.

Bible critics pointed to various contradictions, inconsistencies and terminological variations of the Biblical text as evidence for the documentary hypothesis. They claim that the Bible represents a compilation of various texts composed in various different periods, which later on were assembled by different editors.

Those who believe that the Bible is a product of supernatural communication will find other solutions to the alleged difficulties and contradictions encountered within the Biblical text. The documentary hypothesis became necessary only for those who started out with the presupposition that all phenomena must be explained purely in naturalistic terms, which *a priori* rules out the possibility that any form of verbal communication can take place between God and man.

The emphasis upon individual responsibility for our choice of categories for the interpretation of the data of our experience by no means delegitimizes the role of reason. A comparison with ethical issues may be helpful.

It is widely held by such ethical theories as prescriptivism, emotivism and intuitionism that reason cannot generate our basic moral commitments or beliefs. This, however, does not mean that reason does not play any role in ethics. At the very least, we need to examine the consistency of various ethical beliefs and, if found mutually incompatible, make revisions in the light of critical analysis.

Similarly, our decision to allow non-rational factors to determine beliefs in matters affecting religious faith does not entail our adoption of the extreme position of a Tertullian, who maintained that reason is totally irrelevant to religion, because the more absurd a religious belief, the more plausible it is as an article of faith.

Reason and faith

SIGNIFICANTLY, THE MAINSTREAM of the Jewish religious tradition does not erect a wall of separation between reason and faith. Even Yehudah HaLevi who rejected "natural theology" because the limitations of the human mind compel us to rely exclusively upon Revelation as a source of religious knowledge, took it for granted that no article of faith can contradict the canons of rationality.[89] While he maintains that religious knowledge cannot be grounded in reason, he also unequivocally declares that it cannot contain anything contradictory to reason.

Many medieval Jewish philosophers were so convinced of the validity of rational criteria and their applicability to Revelation that they insisted that Biblical statements which run counter to the dictates of rationality must not be taken literally.[90] For example, they agreed that Biblical statements which attribute corporeal features to God must be interpreted metaphorically.

At the same time it must not be forgotten that the attempts of Jewish rationalists to prove the existence of God by purely rational arguments reflect the pre-critical acceptance of reason as the paramount device for the apprehension of the nature of reality. Nowadays, however, this approach is generally taken as obsolete, because we take it for granted that sense perception alone, not reason by itself, can be the source of empirical knowledge yielding information about matters of fact.

Rejection of proofs for the existence of God must, however, not be confused with the advocacy of an unsophisticated, simplistic approach to matters of faith. Even in our highly skeptical age there is room for the position of a number of traditional Jewish thinkers that belief in God should be treated not just as an act of faith but as a form of knowledge. Thus Bahyah Ibn Pakudah cited the verse "Know the God of your fathers"[91] as prooftext for the need to utilize our intellect in the quest for God.[92] Maimonides believed that Abraham, the model of piety, discovered monotheism after a prolonged intellectual effort to understand the universe.[93] In addition, Maimonides formulated the commandment mandating faith in God not as a commandment to believe but to *know* that there is a God.[94]

Role of the so-called proofs for the existence of God

ACCORDING TO MAIMONIDES, it is imperative that believers be aware that it is the existence of God that makes possible the existence of creatures.

From this premise it follows that, although the limitations of the human mind may prevent us from proving rationally the validity of our belief system, we nonetheless must aspire to relate our theistic beliefs to the entire gamut of our beliefs about the world. This is why the proofs for the existence of God retain significance even for those who are persuaded by Kant that they are not cogent. What we can learn from the various proofs is how to relate our theological beliefs to our experiences of the world, be they the realm of nature, ethics or aesthetics.

The cosmological argument, for example, shows the theist how to synthesize belief in the validity of the laws of nature with the tenets of monotheism. Seen through the eyes of faith, the cosmos becomes the realm of Divine creation.

Nature is viewed as the domain in which the operation of the various laws governing the sequence of phenomena conceals the presence of God. This approach is already anticipated in the observation of the Talmud that the Hebrew word for world, *Olam*, also denotes concealment.[95]

In a similar vein, the Zohar notes that when we rearrange the letters forming *Mi Eleh* (Who are these?), we obtain the word *E-lohim* (God of nature and justice). Rav Shneur Zalman of Liadi developed this concept when he suggested that the numerical value the Hebrew term *teva* (nature) is identical with that of E-lohim. Thus it is accepted that the probing eye of faith will discover the God Who is hidden in the natural world.

To turn to other examples of the use of inconclusive proofs for the existence of God, the argument from Design confirms the thesis of Psalm 104 that the structure, order and harmony of the universe attest to the wisdom of the Creator. As summed up in verse 24, "How manifold are Thy works, Oh Lord, in wisdom hast Thou made them all, the world is full of Thy possessions." Along similar lines, the ontological proof enables us to grasp that the mode of God's existence is so unique that it cannot be compared with the existence predicated of any creature or entity.

Even Kant's moral proof, for all its weaknesses, can be utilized by believers to relate their moral experience (especially its overridingness of all other considerations) to the belief that the moral "ought" represents a Divine imperative. But all these formulations are possible only when we begin our search with the faith that there is a God and subsequently seek to relate our various experiences to this fundamental belief.

That this kind of sophisticated faith is superior to the simplistic faith of the naive believer is far from being an innovation of philosophically minded thinkers like Bahyah Ibn Pakuda or Maimonides. It was already suggested in the Biblical statement: "From there you will seek the Lord, your God, and you shall find Him, if you search after Him with all your heart and all your soul."[96] It should be noted that the Torah made our finding God contingent upon all-out efforts to search for Him. This may be why the Sages advised, "Do not believe an individual who claims to have found [spiritual treasures] without having toiled for them."[97]

We can search for Him in many ways. We must begin with refusing to let familiarity dull our sense of wonder. In this search some will follow the lead of an Abraham, who, as Maimonides[98] describes it, was puzzled by the very existence of a universe. It was in the quest to understand the mystery of why there is a world at all that he reached God. Others will rise above the hum-drum routine of daily existence and will question whether there is any meaning to their lives. Searching for an answer they may discover God as the Ground of all value and purpose. Others will probe the mystery of the moral experience and come to the conclusion that only faith in God can adequately account for it.

It must be emphasized that these observations must not be misconstrued. We are a far cry from suggesting that confronting the various mysteries will enable us to rationally infer the existence of God. But we must bear in mind that there is nothing to prevent those who contend that rational knowledge alone cannot lead us to God from agreeing that the more we search for God, the greater the likelihood that we may be able to encounter Him. Faith is not a gratuitous gift, but an achievement wrought by relentless effort.

SEX, LOVE AND FAMILY[99]

IT IS NO COINCIDENCE THAT THE God-centered existence mandated by Judaism has throughout history fostered close family relationships. As the Bible puts it, "It is not good for man to be alone."[100] Self-centered individuals cannot enter into genuine communication with others, let alone establish true community with them. It is not surprising that the atheistic French existentialist Sartre, who declared that "hell is other people" claimed that all human relationships are based upon conflict and that, therefore, love becomes a project that is condemned to failure.

Human versus animal sexuality

JUDAISM, ON THE OTHER HAND, maintains that a proper loving relationship is possible only when the Divine presence creates a bond between human beings.[101] Unlike Sartre, who contended that love is "contact between skins," or Freud, who viewed love as the sublimation of the sexual instinct, Judaism maintains that a purely physical relationship is an abuse of human sexuality, which is designed to create a bond between individuals.

Animals are also endowed with sexual desire. This is necessary to enable them to mate and insure the propagation of the species. But the purpose and function of human sexuality is different. Its objective should be not simply to mate but to achieve "sexual union." As Nachmanides interprets Genesis 2:24, "becoming one flesh" is permissible only after a permanent relationship has been established between the partners. It is only then that the commandment "to be fruitful and multiply" can be properly fulfilled.[102]

It is highly significant that before the expulsion from the Garden of Eden, the Bible declares that humans require a helpmate. At this stage, before human beings were confronted with their own mortality, they felt no need for descendants. Adam called the woman who was formed from his side by the name of *Ishah* (the female gender of *Ish* [male human]). He needed her because he realized that he was incomplete until he was reunited with the missing dimension of his existence. This accounts for the Rabbinic statement that "until a man marries a woman, he cannot be considered complete."[103]

Marriage

FROM THIS PERSPECTIVE, THE sexual impulse is implanted in humans in order to help them overcome their existential loneliness and establish true community with a partner without whom one would not be a complete human being.[104] It therefore is wrong to employ the sexual drive solely for physical gratification and not as a means to express love and to establish a sense of community. A purely mechanical approach to sex cannot result in "love making," but, at best, lead to erotic gratification. Moreover, because human beings bear the image of God, they must not be treated as sexual objects to be manipulated for one's pleasure.

Contrary to Freud and Sartre, love is not a derivative of sex, but rather sexual desire is an instrumentality for making possible the most intimate union between individuals in which one's spouse is regarded as the extension of one's own self.[105]

Because sex is designed to foster this intimacy, Judaism mandates conjugal sexual relations, even when there is no possibility that pregnancy might result. On the other hand, once a couple has decided to terminate a marriage, it is strictly prohibited to engage in sexual relations.

That procreation is not the only purpose of human sexual relations becomes evident also from the Biblical story, which indicates that the desire for offspring arose only after the expulsion from Paradise, when it was made clear to Adam that he will eventually return to the dust from which he was formed. Only then, with the awareness of the inevitability of death, did propagation of the human species become important. This is why he no longer referred to his spouse as Ishah (part of himself) but as *Chavah* (Eve) – mother of all those who live.

As opposed to the current ethos which treats the aim of marriage primarily as the attainment of personal happiness of the spouses, Judaism views marriage not just as a private affair but as an essential requirement for the realization of the transcendent goals and objectives of the Jewish people. This may be the reason why the presence of a *Minyan* (a quorum of ten men which symbolically represents the entire Jewish community) is indispensable to the recital of all the blessings of *Nissuin* (the second part of the wedding ceremony).[106]

The requirement for a Minyan at a wedding ceremony makes the couple aware that their union is not merely a private matter but has communal significance. They are reminded that the prerequisite of marital love – focusing on the well-being of another person – should not be confined to one's spouse but should extend in varying degrees of intensity to other members of the family and the community as well.

Ideally, marital love should be a stepping stone in moving away from preoccupation with self-fulfillment and self-gratification to genuine altruism and commitment to transcendent objectives.

Family bonds should be viewed not as the outer limits of altruism but as the matrices for forming commitment to transcendent values encompassing other fellow human-beings. Perhaps this is what the Rabbis meant when they declared that it is only when the Divine Presence is encountered between husband and wife that they can truly be worthy of each other.[107]

Family and community

To appreciate more fully the enormous importance that Judaism attaches to the institution of marriage, one must view it not in isolation but place it within the context of the communal orientation which characterizes Judaism. Professor A. N. Whitehead's definition of religion as "what man does with his solitariness," may be appropriate for Christianity, but certainly not for Judaism. Whereas Christianity views human spiritual destiny primarily in purely personal terms – the individual human soul in relation to God – Judaism stresses the significance of belonging to the collective entity of the Jewish people, which is charged with the mission of forming "a kingdom of priests and a holy people."[108] Because Jews are related to God not simply as individuals but as members of a natural and historic community – the people of Israel – identification with the Jewish people and experiencing a special sense of kinship and solidarity with all fellow Jews is treated as an indispensable ingredient of Jewish piety.

Jewish conversion procedures reflect this community-centered orientation. They mandate not merely commitment to the tenets of the Jewish faith but also identification with the people of Israel. This is patterned after the Biblical formula as stated in the Book of Ruth: "Your people are my people and your God is my God."[109]

Maimonides goes so far as to brand as a heretic anyone who, however learned in Torah and however meticulous in the observance of religious practices, displays total indifference to the welfare of the Jewish community.[110]

Parental and filial duties

There can be little doubt that the replacement of this value system by a self-centered individualism bears primary responsibility for the current unprecedented erosion of family ties which afflicts modern society. Actually, the disintegration of the family is not an isolated phenomenon, but part of a syndrome of a host of problems which plague us, because we no longer recognize the authority of transcendental norms. Since the canons of modernity dictate that all values must be justified in terms of our own subjective desires, it is no wonder that we suffer from utter permissiveness and the erosion of the very values that make for healthy family relationships. If there are no healthy family relationships, how can we hope to cultivate an atmosphere of true community? Is not the logical consequence of looking upon our own sense of self-satisfaction as the criterion of moral propriety that we treat other persons merely as means towards our own self-realization or self-gratification?

Failure to provide a transcendental foundation for our values makes it virtually impossible for parents to function as proper guides for their children. If moral values merely reflect the personal values of parents, it would be unconscionable for them to burden their children with what, in the final analysis, amounts to no more than concern for their own selfish interests. Carried to its logical conclusion, this would rule out the possibility of providing children with a proper upbringing, since education must involve more than the transmission of skills or factual information. There can be no value-free education, since education is supposed to be a preparation for life and one cannot live without making evaluations. Hence, education must provide standards by which choices and decisions are to be made.

Traditionally, Jews refer to their parents as their teachers, because parents are viewed not as pals, but as teachers, who are charged with the responsibility to instruct their children in the value-system of the community.

The Fifth Commandment, usually translated as "Honor thy father and thy mother" actually demands more than respect and honor. The Hebrew term *kabbed*, is usually translated as 'honor' but it actually is derived from the Hebrew *kaved* which means heavy. Hence the Hebrew word kabbed implies that one should attach weight to the impact of one's parents and give them a substantial role in the moulding of our lives, even beyond their own lifetime. They should be revered as authority figures whose values we are obliged to respect, provided they do not conflict with the transcendental values of the community.

The Torah instructs us, "Ask thy father and he will declare to thee, thy elders and they will tell thee."[111] Parents are granted a special status entitling them to respect and reverence as authority figures in order to enable them to discharge their duty to instill within their children a commitment to the values of the Jewish community.

Obviously, this outlook clashes head-on with the canons of the "open society," which categorically reject the thesis that belonging to a particular group or family is a valid reason for the acceptance of its norms or values. According to the ethos of the "open society," one must opt for values solely on the basis of independently arrived at "rational" considerations – not because of the accident of birth."[112]

Judaism, however, maintains that a genuinely free life must nurture the natural sentiments of family bonds, group solidarity and attachment to community. Notwithstanding its insistence upon equal regard for all individuals,[113] Judaism recognizes the importance of special relations. For example, we are mandated to give preferential treatment to the poor of our own community before those of another community.[114] For that matter, we are obligated to tend to the needs of our own family before those of non-relatives. Similarly, while all of human life is sacred and we must not dismiss as trivial even the death of total strangers, a period of mourning is required only for the loss of close relatives.

The importance which Judaism attaches to the identification with a community can also be gauged by the fact that the Passover *Seder,* which epitomizes the Jewish approach to education, links the celebration of freedom with induction into a community. It is through the community that the hierarchy of transcendental values is mediated to individuals, providing them with a meaningful structure for living.

Viewed from a Jewish perspective, the fact that human beings are endowed with numerous social impulses shows that human nature involves the capacity for self-transcendence. That total self-centeredness goes against human nature can also be seen from the amazing phenomenon that for all their ethical and cultural diversity, all societies have in common those moral norms which protect the life and property of other members of their own group.

Building upon this foundation, Judaism declares that without commitment to the ultimate Source of all reality and value, our need for self-transcendence cannot be adequately satisfied. As the Psalmist reminds us, even the bonds between parents and children cannot last indefinitely. "My father and mother have abandoned me, but God has taken me in."[115] In the final analysis, no human association can fully satisfy our innate need for community.

The close linkage between altruism and religious faith was expressed by the Rabbinic Sages, when they stated that a person who shuns the practice of charity cannot be a true believer in God, but is guilty of idolatry.[116] Perhaps, they referred to the idolatry that Walt Whitman described as "egotheism" – the worship of one's own self.

We thus see that Judaism views our most basic biological urges and psychological drives as evidence of our basic need for self-transcendence. As the Book of Job expresses it, "From my own flesh I behold God."[117] Starting with the sexual instinct through the natural attachment of parents to their offspring to the sense of solidarity with community, we possess all kinds of desires that transcend our own selves and point to the need for a relationship with the ultimate Source of all value and being.

THE COVENANT AND THE UNIQUENESS OF THE JEWISH EXPERIENCE

APART FROM THE VARIOUS natural drives which for all human beings may function as "pointers to God," Jews have additional grounds for interpreting specific features of their mentality as avenues leading to God. It is a remarkable trait of the Jewish psyche that even avowedly secular Jews attach extraordinary significance to the retention of their Jewish identity.

Many Jews, who are completely indifferent to Jewish values, nevertheless express a desire to be buried in a Jewish cemetery. Additional evidence of the importance attached to the perpetuation of Jewish identity is provided by the tremendous efforts made even by secular members of the Jewish community to insure its survival.

Purely ethnic or nationalistic sentiments of group loyalty can hardly account for this. It seems far more plausible that below the surface of overt secularism there run deep covert religious currents, which inspire the resolve to promote "Jewish continuity."

Identification with the Jewish community

THAT MANY JEWS VIEW their belonging to the Jewish community as an outright duty underscores the basically religious character of Jewish survival.[118] There is no stigma attached to abandoning one's ethnic group. One suffers no guilt feelings about changing one's cultural milieu or assimilating into a different social environment. But, somehow, leaving the Jewish fold is looked upon as a disgraceful act of apostasy and treachery, which induces all sorts of recriminations and guilt feelings.

Historically, the obligation to remain within the Jewish community was rooted in a clear-cut religious imperative. It derived from the belief that Israel encountered the living God on Mount Sinai, where it entered into a Covenant and obligated itself to become His "chosen people." The power of this faith was so strong that it overcame the temptation to convert from it in order to escape from the dismal conditions of the ghetto. Although conversion to the dominant religion presented the ticket of admission to all social and economic opportunities available in the larger society, few Jews were prepared to pay this price.

Our traditional faith in supernatural Revelation and a Covenant between God and Israel was challenged by the Enlightenment. It undermined the very foundations of the belief that to remain a member of the Jewish people outweighed all other economic, social and political advantages which apostasy might confer. It is, therefore, not surprising that when in the wake of the Emancipation the gates to the larger world were opened, many Jews embraced the advantages of total assimilation into the non-Jewish world. Lacking the will to survive as Jews, they completely severed their connection with the Jewish community. On the other hand, many non-religious Jews were deeply apprehensive over the mass defections and searched for ways to halt the process and to safeguard the viability of the Jewish community.

But why this concern with assimilation, intermarriage and the loss of Jewish self-identification? Some Jewish thinkers follow Ahad Ha'am and attribute this concern to a collective will to survive. But the very conception of a national will to survive rests upon a logical fallacy. It ascribes to the group as a whole the characteristics of its individual members. The will to live or the instinct for self-preservation *prima facie* applies to biological entities. A good many unwarranted assumptions have to be made before we can even carry over the concept to social groups. Small wonder that the historian Yehezkel Kaufmann branded the collective will to survive a sheer "figment of the imagination."[119]

It therefore seems that the concern for the survival of the Jewish community transcends purely ethnic considerations and possesses religious overtones. As Emil Fackenheim expressed it,

"The Jew of today who persists in regarding Jewish survival as a duty, either posits something unintelligible, or else he postulates, however unconsciously, the possibility of a return to the living God."[120]

In a similar vein, Rav Kook welcomed the return of avowedly secularist and atheistic Zionists to the land of Israel as an unconscious act of Teshuvah (return to God).

We must bear in mind that Judaism represents an organic whole which cannot be separated into ethnic and religious components. One cannot be a member of this community of believers without experiencing a sense of kinship and solidarity with its members. Rabbi Joseph B. Soloveitchik explained this by reference to the "Covenant of Abraham," which mandates that Jews form a community of fate as well as of faith.[121]

Communal thrust

THE COMMUNAL THRUST OF JUDAISM also comes to the fore in the numerous laws which were enacted for the purpose of instilling within Israel a sense of uniqueness and distinctiveness. The practice of the Jewish religion, therefore, includes what might be defined as ethnic components. Judaism (Judaic religious values) cannot be divested from Jewishness (ethnic consciousness). The mere fact that a practice is ordained by customary usage automatically endows it with religious authority. An established custom is accorded the same authority as a Torah law. According to the Talmud,[122] the admonition "do not forsake the teaching of thy mother,"[123] mandates compliance with the customs adopted by the people. If necessary, one is obligated, at the cost of one's life, to defy the edict of a government which seeks to uproot distinctive Jewish practices in order to promote assimilation, even if the prohibited custom has no intrinsic value whatsoever.[124] Thus religious value is attached to anything that contributes to the strengthening of identification and solidarity with the Jewish community.

The liturgy also underscores the communal thrust of Judaism. Public worship is preferable to private prayer. Moreover, most of the obligatory prayers are couched in the plural and address communal rather than personal needs. Significantly, a Kabbalistic formula, which is widely recited before the performance of various rituals, proclaims that the act is performed "in the name of all of Israel."

Yehezkel Kaufmann had ample reasons for defining Judaism as a "religious ethnicism." Since universal and particularistic elements are held in dialectical tension with one another, any attempt to force Judaism into the strait jacket of either a universalistic ethics or a particularistic nationalism is bound to lead to a grotesque distortion of its true nature. It therefore should not be surprising that the experience of their Jewishness is for many Jews the beginning of a process, which ultimately leads them to find God.

FAITH AND HISTORY

IT HAS BEEN ARGUED that of all the approaches to religious faith, the most persuasive one is based upon the historic experience of the Jew. Yehudah HaLevi emphasized that in the opening verse of the Decalogue, God is referred to, not as the Creator of the universe, but as the One "Who has taken us out from the land of Egypt and the house of bondage."[125]

Judaism revolves around the belief in a specific historic event – the Revelation on Mount Sinai. Yehudah HaLevi pointed to the sharp contrast between Judaism and other religions. The latter claim that their respective founders received a private Revelation from God, but Judaism revolves upon the belief in a public Revelation witnessed by over six hundred thousand Israelites. According to HaLevi, this in itself is convincing proof of its veracity. For while a claim to be the recipient of a private Revelation is irrefutable, nobody would have dared to fabricate the story that an entire people had witnessed such an event at Mount Sinai,[126] unless the collective memory of the people would corroborate it.

Obviously, for the believer, the Biblical account of the public nature of the Sinaitic Revelation will help reinforce the belief in the Divine origin of the Torah. But for the non-believer it is a far cry from a clear-cut proof. Those who subscribe to the various documentary theories proposed by Bible critics will simply argue that the Biblical version is just a historic myth that was invented many centuries later.

Of late, another argument has been proposed to "prove" the Divine origin of the Torah. It has been claimed that on the basis of statistical evidence, it can be shown that combinations of letters, if properly decoded, accurately predict significant events in Jewish history. On the other hand, prominent Orthodox mathematicians question the cogency of the statistical evidence adduced in support of so called "Torah Codes." This being the case, the Torah Codes, at best, will bolster the faith of the believers that the Torah is Divinely revealed, while non-believers will dismiss the alleged statistical proof of the probability that the Torah represents the word of God.

The unique historic experiences of the Jewish people are also offered by Nachmanides[127] as evidence of the Divine origin of the Torah. Noting that chapter 32 of Deuteronomy accurately predicts the destiny of the Jewish people, he sees in it a guarantee of the eventual Redemption of Israel. But here again it must be pointed out that, while the accuracy of the predictions will reinforce the faith of believers, a confirmed secularist will not abandon his conviction because of this kind of evidence. Over the centuries, there have been individuals such as Leonardo DaVinci or Jules Verne, who forecast correctly events that most people regarded at that time as being completely beyond the realm of possibility.

The very survival of the Jewish people in the face of horrible conditions and murderous hostility is frequently treated as a mystery that defies rational explanation. Especially noteworthy is the comment of Voltaire, who, when asked why, for all his skepticism, he still believed in God, replied: "Had it not been for the miracle of the survival of the Jewish people, I would have given up this belief as well."

A modern Jewish philosopher, Isaac Breuer, also invokes the inexplicable mystery of Jewish history as proof for the divinity of the Torah. He is struck by Chapters 26 of Leviticus and 28 of Deuteronomy, which accurately foretell the dismal conditions of the Diaspora, the survival of the people in the face of overwhelming odds, the attachment of Jews to the land of Israel after close to two thousand years of exile, and the persistence of anti-semitism, regardless of the economic or social status of Jews or whether they assimilate or stubbornly cling to their distinctiveness.[128]

The State of Israel

HAD BREUER WRITTEN AFTER THE establishment of the State of Israel, he surely would have added the "miracle," that after enduring the horrors of the Holocaust, the Jewish people succeeded in rising from the ashes to create a sovereign Jewish State. What made this amazing feat even more incomprehensible is the fact that it did not make sense for secular Jews, who suffered so much on account of their Jewish ancestry, to be so concerned with the perpetuation of their Jewish identity, instead of assimilating completely into their surrounding societies.

For Breuer, these baffling phenomena would defy explanation by natural causes. The various explanations of ordinary historic phenomena cannot account for the inexplicable events of our history. As the Sages put it, Jewish history is not subject to the laws of causality.[129] It is evidence of the meta-historic nature of the Jewish people. For Breuer, not metaphysics, but meta-history is the road leading to the recovery of Judaism.[130]

In recent years, this approach has gained many adherents, especially among the ranks of those traditional Jews who see in the establishment of the State of Israel an "overt miracle" wrought by God, proof that we are witnessing the dawn of the Messianic era. They believe that the triumphs of the Six Day War, the development of Jerusalem into a truly metropolitan center of Jewish life, the mass *Aliyah* from Russia, especially after the toppling of the Communist empire, all reveal, in a special and unique manner, that God operates in history.

Although many traditionalists are persuaded that they hear "the footsteps of the Messiah" in these events, I am wary of all eschatological perspectives. Unless endowed with the gift of prophecy, human beings cannot fathom the meaning of the Divine design for history. Obviously, as a believing Jew, I am committed to the proposition that God acts in history. But that does not mean that I can pick and choose events to cite as concrete evidence in order to try to convince a secularist that the establishment and development of the State of Israel can only be explained in terms of Divine miraculous intervention.

The Purim miracle represents, in Jewish literature, the paradigm not of an overt but of a hidden miracle. It goes without saying that religiously sensitive individuals attribute every occurrence to God's acting in history. For that matter, every natural phenomenon, no matter how ordinary and regular or destructive, should be perceived as a manifestation of Divine wisdom and benevolence. In the words of the Psalmist, "The heavens proclaim the glory of God."[131] Maimonides castigates those who fail to perceive calamities and tragedies as a summons to repentance, but dismiss them as mere chance events totally unrelated to God's acting in history.[132]

Obviously, not all events are equally suited to evoke a religious response. The hand of God can be more readily perceived in some events rather than others. While the Holocaust undermined religious faith, the resurgence of Israel buttresses it.

The very existence of Israel as a sovereign state helps confirm the faith of a believer. With the return of a large number of Jews to the land of Israel, the belief in the restoration of our national home and in the "Ingathering of the Exiles" – vital ingredients of the Messianic tenets – has become much more plausible than it was in the pre-state era. When Herzl first proposed his "Jewish State," the idea struck many as so unrealistic that they questioned his sanity. Had there been only a Holocaust but no Jewish State, many Jews would have found it impossible to believe in the possibility of an "Ingathering of Exiles," let alone of an ultimate Redemption.[133] Hence, for all its precariousness and deficiencies, the very existence of a sovereign Jewish State in itself, regardless of what the future may hold, confirms our faith in the feasibility of the Messianic ideal.

It must be emphasized that the position advanced here is totally free of any pseudo-Messianic elements. I wholeheartedly hope and pray that the State of Israel will develop into a Messianic State. But a prayer is not a prognosis. I was highly impressed by the suggestion of Rabbi Yitzchak Nissim, late Chief Rabbi of Israel, that the State of Israel should be characterized as "the test of our worthiness for Redemption" rather than, as formulated in the current prayer for the State, "the beginning of the sprouting forth of our Redemption."

I am prepared to attach Messianic significance to the State of Israel only in the same limited fashion as our Sages did to the Maccabean victory. We find that the Sages were hardly enamored with the Maccabees. The Book of Maccabees was not admitted into the Holy Writ and there are very few references to Chanukah in the entire Talmud. Moreover, the achievements of the Maccabees were only of limited duration. Jewish sovereignty over the Land was short-lived and the Temple was destroyed by the Romans. Yet these shortcomings did not prevent the Sages from attributing Messianic significance to the accomplishments of the Maccabees, as evidenced by the fact that they chose for the Haftorah reading on the Sabbath of Chanukah a selection from the Prophet Zechariah,[134] which refers to the Messianic era.[135]

We ought to react in a similar fashion to the establishment of the State. While we have no guarantees for the future, we should hail its existence as a remarkable opportunity to advance our Messianic ideals – the rule of God over our individual and collective lives. The attainment of Jewish sovereignty provides us, for the first time in almost two thousand years, with the opportunity to conduct our socio-political, economic and military activities in accordance with the Divine will as formulated in the Halakhah.

It must, however, be borne in mind that this approach to the re-establishment of a sovereign Jewish State represents merely a subjective opinion. There is a minority within traditional circles that looks askance at the formation of a Jewish State, let alone one with a secular orientation, before the arrival of the Messiah. They denounce the establishment of the State of Israel as the "handiwork of Satan," designed to sway Jews from the course mandated by God."[136] In their judgment all human initiatives aiming at the restoration of Jewish sovereignty are absolutely forbidden because only direct Divine intervention can end the blight of Galut, which is punishment for our sins.

We thus see that it is highly problematic to base faith in God on the evidence of Jewish history. True, Isaiah[137] assigns to Israel the function of bearing witness to the existence of God. But it is only when we view history with the eyes of faith that we can discern in it the hand of God.

To present history as objective evidence for the existence of God to a non-believer is an exercise in futility. Like most theological arguments, they are unnecessary for the believer, and useless for the non-believer. But, as we already observed with respect to various other "proofs" of the existence of God, they are of great help to the believer in the quest to relate the insights of faith to the unfolding of the historic process.

THE PROBLEM OF EVIL AND THE HOLOCAUST

ALTHOUGH WE HAVE ADMITTED that no purely intellectual demonstration of God's existence is feasible, we still must address the troublesome argument that the existence of evil in the world actually disproves the existence of God. The challenge has become especially acute in the wake of the Holocaust, which robbed so many survivors of their faith in a benevolent God. It is not surprising that the issue of the compatibility of religious belief with the suffering and pain encountered in the world has evoked greater interest than any other theological issue.

Actually, the problem has two components: 1) the distribution of suffering and pain which is traditionally defined as the problem of the suffering of the righteous and 2) the very existence of evil in itself. Significantly, both the Bible and Rabbinic literature only deal with 1), while completely ignoring 2), which during antiquity was encountered only in secular literature.

Divine justice and the distribution of evil

ABRAHAM CHALLENGED GOD'S INTENTION to destroy Sodom not on the ground that it would be a horrendous calamity but because he believed it would be a violation of justice.[138] What troubled him was not the suffering inflicted upon the inhabitants, but that the innocent and the guilty would share the same fate, which would be incompatible with Divine justice. Similarly, Job did not raise any objection to the existence of evil in the form of suffering and pain, but challenged God on the ground that *his* suffering was completely undeserved. The Psalmist, too, was fully reconciled to the existence of evil. But what almost caused him to lose his faith in God was the prosperity of the wicked, which gave rise to the impression that God was ignorant of human affairs.[139] Thus we note that the only questions raised about evil in the Bible are related to the belief in Divine justice which is challenged by what appears to be an unfair distribution of pain and evil in the world.

Rabbinic literature took for granted the need for reward and punishment. Since the latter is impossible without inflicting some experience of pain or loss, the existence of some evil is inevitable. The main concern of the Rabbis was to insure that the existence of evil would not be interpreted in terms of dualism, which attributed the existence of evil to forces arrayed against God. The Rabbis unequivocally affirmed Isaiah's thesis that "[God] forms light and creates darkness, makes peace and creates evil."[140] It is interesting that when they included this verse in the daily liturgy, the Rabbis modified the text slightly by substituting for the word *evil* the less offensive *everything*. Apparently, they were reluctant to ascribe the authorship of evil to God, since they were convinced that "whatever God does, is for the good."[141] The Midrash even looks upon the existence of death and suffering as the reasons why the universe is pronounced by the Bible not merely as "good," but "very good."[142]

The very existence of evil as a challenge to faith

IT WAS ONLY AFTER THE APPEARANCE of Epicurus that we encounter within non-Jewish sources the argument that the very existence of evil refutes theism, which defines God as the absolutely perfect Being, Whose perfection entails that He is both omnipotent and omnibenevolent. It is argued that an omnibenevolent God would seek to prevent the evil of suffering and pain as much as possible. But if God is also omnipotent, He could eliminate all forms of evil. Hence, the presence of evil in the world entails the non-existence of God.

Professor Alvin Plantinga,[143] however, has demonstrated the fallacy of this argument. While it follows that God should prevent all *unnecessary* evil, He may have good reason to create evil, when, by doing so, the world would become more perfect than it would be without it. This is the case when the existence of that evil created or condoned by God would be necessary for the attainment of the greatest possible good.

Over the centuries numerous theodicies have been advanced to explain why various forms of evil are necessary. They all seek to explain why, without the presence of various forms of evil, the world would be less perfect. Actually, as Professor Plantinga has argued, we need not know why any particular evil is necessary. Regardless of whether we can explain how an evil contributes to the greatest possible good, our faith in an omnipotent and omnibenevolent God assures us that whenever we encounter any form of evil, from a Divine perspective it must be a necessary form of evil, although humans may fail to understand its necessity.

The only time we really must fall back upon theodicies is when we employ the Argument from Design for the purpose of demonstrating the existence of God. This highly popular argument for theism contends that the complex structure of the universe, in which the various constituent parts fit together harmoniously to sustain life, proves conclusively that the world was designed by an omnipotent and omnibenevolent God.

Were someone to present the counter-argument that the evil, suffering and maladjustment we encounter in the universe refute the belief that the world is so perfectly arranged that it must have been created by an omnipotent and omnibenevolent God, we cannot simply dispose of this objection by claiming that the presence of evil is necessary to make this the best possible world. Instead, we must be prepared to explain why particular forms of evil are needed to make this a better world than it would have been without their existence. To do so, we would have to employ the various theodicies that have been developed for this purpose.

False arguments that explain evil

AN ENTIRELY DIFFERENT SITUATION prevails, however, when belief in God does not rest on an inference from the properties of the universe (Argument from Design or other cosmological arguments). When our theistic belief represents an act of faith, we can dispense with all theodicies. The so-called problem of evil can be dismissed by stating that if an omnipotent and omnibenevolent God has created the world, all the apparent flaws and imperfections must be necessary from a Divine perspective, although our limited understanding does not enable us to perceive the reasons for their necessity.

One of the most prominent theodicies is the "Free Will Defense." It maintains that human beings can be free only if they have the capacity to make moral choices, which presuppose the ability to choose between good and evil. Hence, the capacity to cause harm and pain is indispensable to the greater good of having a world which contains creatures possessing the dignified status of autonomous beings.

This explanation, however, suffers from serious flaws. To begin with, it does not account for the entire domain of natural evil, such as earthquakes, hurricanes, floods and other catastrophes. Moreover, while the existence of some evil would be necessary for the capacity to make moral choices, it would hardly be necessary to have such enormous quantities of evil in the world, since even a small quantity of evil would suffice for this.

A similar objection could be advanced against the often cited argument that the existence of evil is necessary, because without it, we could not appreciate the good. Here, too, we cannot help but ask, would not a much smaller quantity of evil have sufficed to show the distinction between good and evil?

The same criticism can be levelled against another brand of theodicy, which goes back to Plato and Plotinus, which has been labeled by John Hick "the aesthetic theme."[144] We are like people ignorant of painting who complain that the colors are not beautiful everywhere in the picture, although the artist has lain on the appropriate tint to every spot.[145]

But this solution, too, is inadequate. Even if some evil is necessary for aesthetic reasons, the question still remains why do we require so much evil to make the universe truly beautiful?

Another popular brand of theodicy, the so called "Soul-Making Argument," can also be subjected to similar objections. The existence of evil is defended on the ground that without it such important values as sympathy, empathy and compassion would not be possible. But even were we to grant that the existence of these values would outweigh the price to be paid for them in terms of evil, we would still have to explain why such great amounts of evil as afflict our world would be necessary.

Some of the theodicies advanced by classical Jewish thinkers also fail to satisfy the modern mind. Thus Maimonides argues that any form of existence is a good. What we experience as evil is merely a privation of some good, but not a form of evil. Somehow, we would balk at consoling parents whose child is born with a severe congenital disease by assuring them that they are not confronting evil but merely the absence of some good.

Maimonides also contends that the universe as a whole is good, because of the preponderance of good over evil. Although frequently the laws of nature are the source of evil, in the long run they produce far more good than evil.[146]

This explanation that the smaller quantity of evil, which necessarily results from the operation of the laws nature, is justified by the greater balance of good we observe in the world, however, makes sense only as long as we adhere to the rationalistic conception that the laws of nature are based upon rationality. Just as the belief in Divine omnipotence is not challenged by the argument that God could not create another omnipotent God, or, for that matter, a stone which He could not lift, because omnipotence does not involve the capacity to do what is logically impossible, so God could not have created laws of nature which do not conform to the requirements of rationality.

But this explanation presupposes the validity of the Aristotelian philosophy of nature, which has been rejected in the modern world. Nowadays, it is taken for granted that all laws of nature have no rational basis but are merely contingent. Hence, we could ask why did not an omnipotent, benevolent God create different laws of nature which do not give rise to any evil, let alone such enormous quantities.

Apart from these specific objections, we also may question the justice of defending the suffering of an individual because it is necessary for the greatest possible good. We cannot help but agree with Kant that the explanations of theodicies are like cures that are worse than the diseases themselves.

Difficulties with the notion of the best possible world

PROFESSOR GEORGE SCHLESINGER[147] has persuasively argued that the very notion of the greatest possible good is a logical impossibility. No matter how much goodness the universe contains, it would always be possible to conceive of a universe that would contain an even greater amount of good. Hence, we cannot question why there is any evil in the world, because even if there was no pain and suffering, we still could ask the unanswerable question, why does not an omnipotent and omnibenevolent God confer supreme bliss upon even more beings?

It is for this reason that, according to Professor Schlesinger, the Bible and the Talmud do not raise the problem why is there any evil at all, but confine themselves to examining whether the distribution of good and evil conforms to the requirements of justice.

Rabbi Joseph B. Soloveitchik[148] adopts the Kantian approach and dismisses the entire enterprise of theodicy on the ground that the human mind is not equipped to deal with metaphysical issues. It, therefore, makes no sense to ask: why is there evil in the world? Instead, we should question how best to address the challenge of responding properly to the existence of evil.

It is our task to respond to evil in such a manner that it is converted into a source of good. Thus, personal suffering should be utilized for the purpose of catharsis, of making us more sensitive to the needs of others or inducing within ourselves a sense of contrition conducive to spiritual growth. Moreover, the very existence of pain and suffering enables us to carry out our mission to strive for the elimination of evil – the ethical task of humanity. Accordingly, the universe was left by God in an unfinished state in order to provide human beings with the opportunity of becoming His partners in the creation of the universe.

We can thus readily see that the presence of evil in the world can by no means be adduced as evidence that the belief in an omnipotent and omnibenevolent God is untenable. Contrary to Reconstructionists, who, because of their commitment to a shallow naturalism have adapted William James' notion of a "limited God," we see no compelling reason to abandon theism, which for more than two millennia has managed to survive the onslaught on its tenets brought about by the experience of pain and suffering.

The Holocaust

OF LATE, SOME THINKERS are calling for a radical overhauling of all Jewish theology because the traditional "answers" to the problem of evil cannot explain the enormity of the suffering during the Holocaust.[149] Others contend that, while psychologically, the enormity of "radical evil" in the Holocaust creates unique difficulties, logically the theological questions are not affected by the quantity of evil involved. One child born with a congenital disease presents the same challenge to God's benevolence and justice as millions of children brutally massacred in concentration camps.

From a logical point of view the unspeakable tragedy of the Holocaust does not pose a special threat to theistic belief. We can still maintain that for reasons beyond our comprehension God's plan for the world includes such colossal evil. But the Holocaust has made it almost impossible to defend the "Argument from Design," which postulates the existence of a benevolent God in order to account for the harmony, structure and purposefulness of the universe.

To advance such an argument after the Holocaust, we must be able to show how all the suffering was necessary. But I am repelled by the various "explanations" offered as reasons for the occurrence of this abysmal tragedy. I cannot accept the argument that the Holocaust was deserved punishment for our sins. Were those who survived the horrors spiritually superior to those who perished in the gas chambers? What was the guilt of the babies who perished in the ovens of the crematoria? Were American Jews more noble and worthy of being saved than their brothers and sisters in Europe?

By the same token, I categorically reject the "solution," which purports to "justify" the Holocaust on the ground that it made possible the establishment of the State of Israel. To me such an explanation borders on the blasphemous. How can anyone maintain that the achievement of a sovereign state outweighed the unspeakable horrors of the Holocaust and the annihilation of six million Jews, who represented the most important reservoir of Jewish intellectual, cultural and religious strength? It is better to admit lack of understanding than to give implausible answers.

Apart from the general theological problem of evil, the Holocaust also poses a specific difficulty for Judaism: can we still believe in a God Who has chosen Israel for a unique mission in history?

But is this really a novel problem? It was already addressed by the prophets of old, who insisted that the destruction of Jerusalem and its Temple was merely a temporary phenomenon and did not constitute a revocation of God's Covenant with Israel. In his *Kuzari*, a treatise which has as its subtitle *An Apology for a Despised Faith*, Yehudah HaLevi also points out that the suffering endured by Israel is due to its central role in the redemptive process[150] – not a sign of rejection by God, as was argued by the Church Fathers.

Unfortunately, some thinkers have been afflicted with failure of nerve and follow Richard Rubenstein in contending that after Auschwitz we can no longer believe in a God Who has a unique relationship with Israel. But it appears to me that the arguments employed with respect to the feasibility of theistic belief in the face of evil, can also be applied to the specific Jewish facets of the problem.

It must be borne in mind that we do not advance the doctrine of God's election of Israel as an explanation for a number of puzzling historic phenomena. Instead, our acceptance of the doctrine represents an act of faith that makes us look upon our unique role in history as a mystery. Problems can be solved, but mysteries can only be apprehended.

From the perspective of faith, both the suffering of the Jewish people during the Holocaust and its rising from the ashes to create a sovereign Jewish State are different facets of the mystery of Jewish existence. The more we contemplate it, the more mysterious it becomes.

CULTIVATION OF FAITH

THANKS TO THE POPULARITY of Martin Buber's writings, it has become a commonplace that the Jewish concept of faith radically differs from that of Christianity. *Emunah,* the Hebrew term for faith, is not the equivalent of the Greek *pistis*, which refers to the belief in dogmas which play such a dominant role in the Gospels. Emunah involves much more than mere assent to doctrines or dogmas. This becomes especially evident when we recall the Biblical verse, usually rendered as "Israel saw the great hand of God...and they believed in the Lord."[151] But this translation does not accurately reflect the meaning of the word *vaya'aminu* of the Hebrew text. This term refers to someone merely "believing in" or "believing that." However, we usually do not use the expression "we believe something" for something which we actually see.

Emunah as faithfulness

ACTUALLY, EMUNAH (the noun which has the same root as the verb vaya'aminu) denotes confirmation, as is the meaning of the term *Amen.* By employing the expression vaya'aminu, the Bible tells us is that seeing the hand of God inspired Israel to commit itself to Him. Additional evidence that the term emunah refers to unwavering commitment and steadfast perseverance, rather than to intellectual belief, is found in Exodus 17:12, where the term emunah describes the steadiness of the hands of Moses after they were supported by Aaron and Hur.

When the prophet Habakkuk extols "the righteous person who lives by his faith",[152] he does not refer to the acceptance of dogmas but rather to the *faithfulness* and steadfastness in governing one's life by spiritual and moral convictions. There are numerous passages in the Bible[153] which extols the Emunah of God. It would be absurd to ascribe to an omniscient God the attribute of operating on the basis of mere faith. It is therefore abundantly clear that in Biblical passages the proper translation of emunah is not "faith" but "faithfulness." A faith versus works controversy, which has divided Christianity, would be unthinkable in Judaism, since emunah is supposed to manifest itself in the conduct of our lives. Thus, as we noted previously, a self-centered individual who affirms belief in God but refrains from the practice of charity is regarded by the Talmud as an idolater.[154] Similarly, the Talmud asserts that regardless of one's profession of belief in a Creator, public desecration of the Sabbath is construed as denial of the belief in Divine Creation.[155]

The action-centered thrust of Judaism manifests itself in an interesting detail of the Jewish liturgy. Continuing our earlier discussion on the Shema, in general, we do not interrupt the reading of a Biblical text with extraneous material. But, as we noted previously, during the recital of the Shema, right after the proclamation of the unity of God, "Hear, oh Israel, the Lord is our God, the Lord is one," we insert the prayer, "May the name of the glory of His Kingdom be blessed for ever." This shows that it is not enough to affirm the existence and unity of God. To be meaningful, this belief must engender within us the resolve to help bring about the realization of His rule in the world. Articulation of the belief in the unity of God is expected to instill, within the worshipers, love and fear of God, and challenge them to direct the various facets of their personality towards the service of God. It was hoped that by striving towards this ultimate goal human beings would be on the road towards overcoming all inner conflict, leading to the emergence of truly harmonious personalities.

The methodology of Judaism

THE TEXT OF THE SHEMA, which is recited after the affirmation of the unity of God, refers to the next step. After the acceptance of the creed it is vital to translate this belief into the love of God and the study, teaching, and observance of His commandments.[156] The Rabbis believed that observance of the Torah was not merely the proper conclusion to be drawn *from* faith but also could serve as the most reliable avenue *to* religious faith. This is why they attributed to God the declaration "Would that they had abandoned Me, but kept my Torah..."[157]

This statement, however, must not be misconstrued as an endorsement of a religious behaviorism which completely discounts the value of the inner life of an agent. Had the Rabbis been so legalistically minded as to concern themselves exclusively with meticulous adherence to the Law, they would not have added the phrase, "because the light of the Torah would eventually have restored them to the right way." What they meant to convey was their conviction that eventually the study and practice of Torah is bound to engender genuine faith.

It is perhaps for this reason that the liturgy contains the prayer, "enlighten our eyes with Thy Torah and attach our heart to Thy commandments, and unite our hearts to love and fear Thy name." The sequence sheds light on the methodology of Judaism. Torah and Mitzvot are considered as the ladder upon which we ascend to reach for ever higher levels of authentic faith. This is why the Talmud sings the praises of Israel for having committed themselves to the Torah with the formula, "We shall do and we shall hear."[158] It is through fulfillment of the commandments that we become attuned to God so that we may truly hear His message.

There is, however, an exception to this rule. At the time of the Sinaitic Revelation, the entire people directly encountered the Presence of God. In the opinion of Maimonides, only Moses was capable of comprehending the content of the Decalogue. Because the rest of the people were not intellectually prepared for prophecy, they had to be satisfied with the awareness that they had encountered God's presence without having an inkling of the meaning of the Voice they heard.

But this kind of encounter is rare. It happens only in the extraordinary situations when God Himself initiates the communication in the form of supernatural Revelation. The normal pattern follows the reverse order. We begin with the content of the Divine Revelation in the Torah and hope that eventually we may reach the goal of a direct encounter with God. As Rav Joseph Soloveitchik formulated it, at the beginning of the study of Torah we aim at the understanding of its ideas. But we hope that immersion in Torah will eventually lead to an encounter with His Presence.[159]

This is probably what Franz Rosenzweig had in mind when he coined the famous adage that "law must become commandment." Ideally, the performance of a Mitzvah should be a response to being addressed by what one believes to be a Divine Commandment. But Judaism does not disparage a good deed which is performed routinely or motivated by ulterior motives. Its primary concern is for actual compliance with the letter of the law. Even in the absence of the awareness that we are responding to God's will, the performance of a mitzvah, still retains *some* religious value. In the words of the Rabbis, even religious commandments that are originally performed with ulterior motives may at least become habits and may ultimately be inspired by nobler motives.[160] At any rate, Judaism emphasizes the primacy of strict adherence to the provisions of the Halakhah, while the quality of the motivations or intentions plays only a secondary role.[161]

For all his preoccupation with the cultivation of the intellect, Maimonides adopted the Aristotelean view that traits of character can only be changed through the modification of conduct. He explains the Rabbinic statement that "the reward of a Mitzvah is another Mitzvah"[162] by noting that the performance of actions molds the personality. Because of the residual effect, the performance of one Mitzvah facilitates the performance of another one. Unfortunately, the reverse is also true regarding undesirable actions.[163] The *Sefer Hachinukh* emphasizes very strongly that the Torah assigns prime value to actions because of their impact upon the formation of attitudes and beliefs.

There may be an even deeper reason why Judaism revolves around the regulation of conduct by Halakhah. As Martin Buber frequently pointed out, Judaism does not seek the dissolution of a finite self in a mystic union with God. A covenantal relationship is possible only when the self is treated as a distinct entity standing in relationship with God. How one *responds* to God's will in one's conduct becomes the ultimate test of piety. As the Shema indicates, the love of God must first of all become manifest in obedience to His explicit instructions. "Thou shalt love the Lord thy God with all thy heart, and with all thy soul, and with all thy might" is immediately followed by "Those words which I command thee today shall be on thy heart."[164]

While obedience to the commandments is a necessary condition of piety, it merely represents the starting point. The highest level of piety is reached only when responding to the Presence of God in every situation becomes the all-encompassing and all-absorbing objective. As Hillel put it, "let all your actions be for the sake of Heaven."[165]

Plurality of reasons for commandments

THAT JUDAISM REVOLVES primarily around conduct rather than ideology becomes also evident upon considering the many conflicting interpretations offered as rationale for the observance of the commandments, *ta'amei hamitzvot*. To begin with, there are sharp divisions of opinion regarding the legitimacy of the entire enterprise of supplying reasons for Divine commandments. Some view it as the height of arrogance for any human being to purport to fathom the reasons for a Divine ordinance. Others, however, maintain that the internalization of the meaning of the commandments is indispensable to deriving maximum benefit from them.[166]

To cite a particularly glaring illustration of the difficulties we encounter in explaining the reason for Divine ordinances, we refer to the commandment (Deut. 22:6-7) that upon finding a bird's nest, one is required to set free the mother bird, while keeping the young ones. There are major disagreements as to the purpose of the Law. One Talmudic source unequivocally declares that it is a Divine decree for which no reason may be offered.[167]

On the other hand, Maimonides, in his *Guide,* contends that this law reflects Divine compassion manifesting itself in the prevention of animal suffering.[168]

Nachmanides,[169] while agreeing that there are reasons for the commandments, disagrees with the specific reason given by Maimonides. He insists that the sole interest of the Torah is to refine and ennoble human beings, not the protection of the animal world. Hence, the law was given for the purpose of preventing the brutalization of human beings as the result of their indifference to the animal world. As opposed to these humanistic explanations, the Gaon of Vilna[170] cites the Zohar, which views the mandated separation of the mother from the young ones as an act of cruelty demanded by God. He compares it to God's request to Abraham to sacrifice his son, Isaac. Hence, the required separation of the motherbird from her young ones indicates that when our most fundamental ethical convictions clash with a Divine commandment, we must be prepared to subordinate all our values to obedience to God's will – a notion strikingly similar to Kierkegaard's "suspension of the ethical."

Incidentally, the differences of opinion concerning the reason why the mother should be sent away is not merely of theoretical interest, but has important practical implications. Relying on the interpretation of Maimonides and Nachmanides, Rav Moses Sofer, widely known as *Chatam Sofer*, concluded that unless one is interested in taking the young birds, it does not make sense to send away the mother.[171] Other authorities differed on the ground that the Torah does not specify any conditions limiting the applicability of the law, and one is therefore obligated to separate the mother from the young ones and send her away in compliance with the Divine ordinance.[172]

Attitudes towards asceticism

THE DIFFICULTIES WE FACE in obtaining guidance on ideological issues from Halakhic data can further be illustrated by a controversy involving the desirability of asceticism. As far back as the Tannaitic period, there was sharp disagreement as to whether the Nazarite's self-imposed asceticism should be commended as meritorious. One view maintained that the reason why the Torah mandated that a Nazarite bring a sin offering upon the termination of the period of abstinence was due to the fact that he had to atone for the sin of unnecessarily having deprived himself of legitimate pleasures.[173] Another opinion adopted the opposite position and argued that reverting back from the exalted status of a Nazarite to the less stringent requirements of ordinary individuals is an act of spiritual regression which necessitates expiation through a sin offering.[174]

The individual and Halakhah

THESE EXAMPLES SHOW THAT various Halakhic data can be interpreted in numerous ways. Just as the same set of postulates can be utilized for geometry and algebra, depending only on what interpretation of the postulates we provide, the Halakhah lends itself to various ideological approaches, reflecting our own individual, subjective preferences.

An analogy from science may be helpful. Modern science made tremendous strides only after it substituted quantitative for qualitative methods. Thus modern physics reduced the world of sounds or colors to wavelengths or quanti. This, of course, did not deny the "reality" of the so called "secondary qualities," such as colors or sounds. But it amounted simply to a methodological device to ignore, for scientific purposes, the entire realm of purely subjective properties. The same "objective" wavelength may produce numerous variations in individual perceptions.

Similarly, the realm of Halakhah represents the "quantitative" aspect of Judaism. It is left to the individual to interpret these objective data in accordance with his/her subjective preferences. Rav Joseph B. Soloveitchik frequently prefaced his philosophical expositions with the *caveat*. "This is how I see it in the light of my own experience. You may avail yourselves of it to the extent that it appeals to you." In other words, while, in his view, an authentic Jewish philosophy must be based upon Halakhic data, identical data may be viewed from a plurality of perspectives, depending upon differences in personality, understanding and ideology of the individuals utilizing the Halakhic framework.

That a variety of ideological positions are compatible with Halakhah can be garnered from the fact that throughout history Jews who professed absolute loyalty to Halakhah adopted radically different life styles and policies. From the battles between rationalists, anti-rationalists and mystics through the controversies dividing Chassidim and Mitnagdim, through the mutually antagonistic positions taken in reaction to the Enlightenment and the Emancipation, to the bitter conflicts raging within the Orthodox community about the legitimacy of Zionism and the State of Israel, Jews have exhibited an uncanny ability to arrive at a host of mutually contradictory conclusions from the same set of Halakhic data.

It must be noted, however, that ideological factors frequently influence the nature of the halakhic data themselves. In my essay, "Meta-halakhic Propositions,"[175] I demonstrated that Halakhic decision-making cannot be completely insulated from subjective considerations. Although there is more latitude accorded to individual idiosyncracies in matters pertaining to Aggada than in Halakhic issues, the difference is one of degree rather than of kind. Rav Samuel Eliezer Edels[176] already pointed out in his classic Talmud commentary that considerable interaction takes place between the two domains. Therefore, one cannot erect an unbreachable wall of separation between an allegedly objective Halakhah and a purely subjective Aggadah.

Since there are numerous disagreements on Halakhic questions, we cannot speak of *the* Halakhah, but in actuality we are confronted with a variety of legitimate Halakhic systems. As long as a Halakhic opinion has evolved in accordance with the methodology governing the development of the "Oral Torah," it represents "the words of the living God."[177] The meaning of a text, as the Deconstructionists remind us, depends upon the reader. Since the Torah "is not in Heaven,"[178] its meaning depends upon the exegesis of human interpreters. This is why the doctrine of the "Oral Torah" maintains that, for normative purposes, the authority for ascertaining the meaning of the Divinely revealed text is vested in fallible human beings, who cannot extricate themselves from the limitations imposed by their respective cultural horizons and divergent subjective perspectives.

It is, however, of the utmost importance that those engaged in determining the meaning of the Torah be not merely scholars, but personalities of exemplary spiritual and moral integrity. It is perhaps for this reason that the thirteen Divine moral attributes, which are supposed to be emulated by human beings, were revealed to Moses immediately before he received the tablets of the Law for the second time. According to Rav Naftali Tzvi Yehudah Berlin,[179] a drastic change occurred with the giving of the second tablets of the law after Israel had worshipped the golden calf. Originally the Written Torah had also included the teachings of the Oral Torah,[180] but now it was different. Israel ceased to be merely a passive recipient, but was assigned an active role in the development of the Oral Torah. In the words of the Sages, it was the responsibility for supplying the Oral Torah that formed the basis of the special Covenant between God and Israel.[181] Since human beings became partners with God in the ongoing creation of the Torah, it was necessary that those who determine its meaning be of superior spiritual stature, lest they wreak havoc with the treasure entrusted to them.

HUMAN INITIATIVES AND MESSIANIC REDEMPTION

THE VARIETY OF INTERPRETATIONS to which the content of Revelation can be subjected becomes even more obvious when we come to grips with the divergent attitudes towards human initiatives that are found in our tradition. On the one hand, we encounter a strong pietistic streak, which extols quietistic acceptance of our fate. It views human efforts as basically irrelevant, because "with the exception of the fear of Heaven, everything is in the hands of Heaven."[182] Any attempt to improve our fortunes would be regarded not only as an exercise in futility but as an act of defiance of God's will. William James went so far as to declare that "the abandonment of self-responsibility" was the hallmark of the religious attitude.[183]

In keeping with this orientation, some authorities maintain that while the Torah grants permission to a physician to attempt to cure a patient,[184] ideally, one should place one's faith in God alone, Who is described in the Torah as "thy Healer" and one should refrain from resorting to medical care. [185]

Pitted against this view are the majority of authorities, who maintain that it is a religious obligation to seek professional medical treatment. Maimonides even rules that a scholar is not allowed to reside in a community which lacks properly qualified medical personnel.[186] In rejecting the argument adduced by his opponents, who opposed recourse to medical science on the ground[187] that God alone is our healer, he points out that by the same logic one might prohibit planting, tilling the soil or even baking bread, because God is described in the Psalms[188] as "He Who giveth bread to all flesh."[189]

According to Maimonides, physicians should realize that they function as God's agents in bringing healing to the sick. Viewed from this perspective, faith in God, far from discouraging human activity, actually serves to prod us to undertake whatever efforts may help to bring about the realization of worthwhile goals. Belief in the need for human action by no means conflicts with the affirmation of Divine omnipotence. Just as God has created a world that follows the laws of nature, so did He create free human beings, to whom He entrusted the task to perfect the universe.

As Rabbi Soloveitchik observed,[190] when the Psalmist declares "Except that the Lord buildeth a house, all the toil of its builders is in vain,"[191] he does not expect that houses will come down ready-made from heaven. But he wants us to realize that ultimately success or failure of our undertakings hinges upon Divine Providence.

Although by now, for all practical purposes, there is complete unanimity that recourse to medical help is not merely sanctioned but represents a religious duty, there are other areas in which pietistic considerations play an enormous role. Influential spokesmen of the Mussar movement counsel quietism and recommend that we devote only a minimal amount of time to earning a livelihood, because our material well-being is solely dependent upon God and not upon our efforts.

Quietism versus activism

THE QUIETISM ENGENDERED BY PIETISM is still felt even more strongly in the approach to collective political efforts of the Jewish community. Originally, large segments of traditionalists were categorically opposed to Zionism, because they felt that only the arrival of the Messiah would end the abnormal conditions under which the Jewish people languished since the destruction of the Temple in Jerusalem by the Romans. To take the initiative towards ending the exile and returning the Jewish people to the land of Israel was viewed as an illegitimate usurpation of Divine prerogatives. The sufferings of the Galut were punishment for our sins, not the result of natural causes. According to the Talmud, the destruction of the Temple was not due to the military superiority of the enemy, but because our own sins had rendered the continued existence of God's sanctuary totally meaningless.[192] By the same token, the blight of Galut can come to an end only with the arrival of the Messiah, whose coming can be hastened only by our own spiritual regeneration.

In opposition to this view, some traditional spokesmen such as Rav Tzvi Hirsch Kalisher, Rav Isaac Jacob Reines, Rav Samuel Mohilever and Rav Kook argued that the belief in a supernatural Messiah does not preclude practical efforts to ameliorate the socio-political conditions of world Jewry through the creation of a national Jewish homeland. But it was only after the Holocaust and the establishment of the State of Israel that the bulk of religious Jewry accepted this position and looked upon the State of Israel as a desideratum.

One must, however, bear in mind that till this very day, a substantial number of Chassidim merely accept the *de facto* existence of the State grudgingly, while others such as the Neturei Karta and the Satmar Chassidim altogether refuse to recognize its legitimacy.[193] In their opinion the establishment of a pre-Messianic Jewish State violated an explicit Talmudic injunction not to take matters into our own hands, warning us against all efforts to bring about the restoration of Jewish sovereignty by force of arms. It is widely accepted that the Messianic hope was largely responsible for the extreme quietism which characterized the mentality of the Jewish community until the Enlightenment. Jews did not struggle for improved socio-political conditions, let alone for the restoration of Jewish independence and sovereignty, because they were sustained by the faith that sooner or later the arrival of the Messiah would spell the end of their suffering. The prevalence of this attitude, as Professor Fackenheim has shown,[194] accounts for Spinoza's contempt for Judaism. He was convinced that because of their religion, Jews displayed utter passivity and made no meaningful attempt to improve their dismal conditions by regaining their independent national existence. Their belief in a miraculous supernatural intervention, which would bring about their Redemption, caused them to rely on prayer and religious rites rather than their own human efforts.

The English playwright George Bernard Shaw succinctly captured this attitude in his *The Little Girl in her Search for God*. In this story, Jews are characterized as a people who instead of resorting to action are simply waiting for God.

Messianism

THE EMINENT HISTORIAN OF JEWISH MYSTICISM, Gershon Scholem even claimed that the belief in the ultimate Redemption through overt Divine intervention makes it impossible to attach real significance to actions performed by ordinary human beings. When the ultimate goal of history is completely in God's hands, so Scholem argues, natural processes can have no relevance for its realization.[195]

But this line of reasoning is by no means convincing. One could easily turn the argument around and maintain that, on the contrary, because it assures us of the ultimate triumph of our cause, belief in the Messianic Redemption strengthens the resolve to cultivate and settle the land of Israel. Moreover, the full import of the Messianic Redemption is not exhausted by the return of Israel to its ancestral homeland, the ingathering of the exiles and the restoration of the central sanctuary on the sacred site of the Temple Mount. It also includes the eventual rejection of paganism and the universal acceptance of monotheism as a prelude to an era of peace, justice and dignity for all of humankind. Such a belief will fortify the dedication to the attainment of these goals for all of humanity on the ground that the assurance of God's eventual intervention in the historic process guarantees that our striving for our ideals will not amount to just a heroic yet futile gesture in pursuit of an unrealizable utopian vision, but will ultimately be crowned with success.

This approach to the Messianic idea bears some similarity to certain implications of Hermann Cohen's Messianic ethics. To be sure, the classical Jewish Messianic belief cannot be reconciled with Cohen's notion that the Messianic era represents an unattainable ethical ideal,[196] not the expectation of an actual historic reality. Yet within the traditionalist camp, which looks upon the actual arrival of a personal Messiah at some point in history as an article of faith, there is also ample support for the thesis that the belief in the ultimate supernatural Redemption by no means disparages human efforts in preparation for the arrival of the Messiah. There are those who contend that the Messiah will finish the task of Redemption, which must be preceded by human initiatives, however inadequate they may be. Thus Rav Tzvi Hirsch Kalischer[197] argued that the supernatural role of the Messiah would begin only after serious efforts were made to reconstitute Jewish life in the land of Israel through resettlement and development of its agriculture by large numbers of Jews.

Rav Menachem Kasher went further than merely looking upon human initiatives as necessary preludes to the ultimate Redemption. He cites a number of sources which refer to the Rabbinic opinion that the Messianic Redemption will have two phases. First, a Messiah from the tribe of Joseph will lead Jews in a battle for control of the land of Israel. But he will fail and will be slain in the war. It will be left to the Messiah of the Davidic Dynasty to successfully finish the task, leading to the triumph of the Jewish people and the establishment of a just and peaceful world order, in which the sovereignty of God will be universally acknowledged. As Rav Kasher pointed out, some authorities interpret this Rabbinic opinion as showing that even unsuccessful efforts to bring about the return of the Jewish people to its ancestral homeland should be included among the activities credited to the Messiah descended from Joseph and, notwithstanding their obvious failure, would qualify as an integral part of the Messianic process.[198]

This doctrine, however, cannot be reconciled with the position of Maimonides, who makes no reference at all to a Messiah belonging to the tribe of Joseph. But this does not mean that Maimonides disparages human efforts to enhance the socio-political conditions of the Jewish people. As a matter of fact, in a famous epistle, he blames the misfortunes of his people on their failure to cultivate martial arts.[199] Moreover, he insists that the Messiah need not perform any miraculous feats to demonstrate his authenticity. It is his success or failure in bringing the entire territory of the land of Israel under Jewish control, resettling the dispersed members of the people of Israel in its ancient homeland and causing them to abide by the Torah that determines whether a particular individual is a genuine Messiah or a pseudo-Messiah. This determination can be made only after the fact. Because these activities do not involve any overt supernatural intervention, it is impossible to be certain initially about the authenticity of a potential Messiah. This is why, according to Maimonides, Rabbi Akiva originally was an enthusiastic follower of Bar Kokhba. It was only the failure of his mission which proved that he was merely a pretender. For Maimonides, a failed Messiah is a self-contradiction.[200]

Since, in this view, activities aiming at the liberation of the Jewish people and at gaining full sovereignty over the land of Israel should be tentatively endorsed and supported as long as there is any realistic hope for success, this interpretation of the Messianic doctrine does not result in a fatalistic reliance upon God's saving acts. On the contrary, it encourages active human participation in the Redemptive process.

Rav Soloveitchik's approach to Messianism

ESPECIALLY NOTEWORTHY IS Rav Joseph B. Soloveitchik's approach to Messianism. On the one hand, he categorically refuses to treat the establishment of the State of Israel as a Messianic event. For all his enthusiasm for an independent Jewish State, he was not even prepared to accord it the preliminary status of *Atchalta De'Geulah* (the beginning of the Redemption). On the other hand, he was unequivocally opposed to the do-nothing passivity of the pietists as they await the arrival of the Messiah.[201]

The key to an understanding of Rav Soloveitchik's attitude towards the religious significance of the State of Israel is provided by his approach to the normative significance of the belief in the eventual Messianic Redemption. Rav Soloveitchik insists that the historical and metaphysical statements of the Bible do not merely convey theoretical truths, but derive their real significance from their important normative implications.

In the chapter, The Search For Meaning and Purpose, I alluded to the important role which the Creation theme occupies in his system. But of equal importance for him is the Redemption theme, which begins with the Exodus from Egypt and concludes with the Messianic Redemption.

> *Halakhic man discerns in every Divine pledge, man's obligation to bring about its fulfillment, in every promise a specific norm, in every eschatological vision an everlasting commandment (the commandment to participate in the realization of the prophecy).*[202]

It can readily be seen that, for Rav Soloveitchik, the promise of a Messianic Redemption, far from inhibiting human action, actually inspires it. According to Rav Soloveitchik, it is precisely because we believe that Israel will ultimately be redeemed by the Messiah that we must do everything within our power to strive for the partial realization of the objectives which can only be fully attained with the arrival of the Redeemer.

> *Redemption is a fundamental category in Judaic historical thinking and experiencing. Our history was initiated by a Divine act of redemption and, we are confident, will reach its finale in a Divine act of ultimate redemption.*[203]

That faith in the ultimate Divine act of redemption does not lead to the devaluation of human activity comes also to the fore in Rav Soloveitchik's emphasis upon the traditional conception of the need for a personal Messiah and his unequivocal rejection of the Reform doctrine of the progressive evolution of a Messianic era.

In his view, the belief in a personal Messiah is vital, because it underscores the importance of the participation of a human agent in the redemptive process. Just as Moses played a pivotal role as an agent of God in the Exodus from Egyptian bondage, so will the ultimate Redemption involve the participation of a human agent as represented by a descendant of the Davidic Dynasty.[204]

WALKING THE MIDDLE GROUND

IN THE LAST TWO CHAPTERS, WE HAVE noted how the Jewish religious tradition can be interpreted in such a variety of ways as to give support both to activism and quietism, to asceticism and the advocacy of experiencing legitimate pleasures. This is due not only to the impact of subjective factors but also to the wide range of polar values which need to be accommodated. Thus we are mandated to cultivate both love and fear of God. Similarly, we should relate to Him both as a transcendent and immanent Being. Moreover, we are confronted with the dialectical tension between Divine justice and mercy, between God the Creator, the author of the impersonal laws of nature, and the Redeemer Who relates to individuals.

The Kabbalistic doctrine of the Divine *Sefirot* (the emanations that made Creation possible) is additional evidence of the need to synthesize opposing values. It inspired an ethics which, stressing the emulation of Divine attributes, calls for the blending of polar values. As opposed to widely held assumptions, Rabbi Soloveitchik argued that the Maimonidean ethical ideal of the "middle road" is not patterned after the Aristotelean model but reflects the requirements of *Imitatio Dei* – the need to harmonize the various polar values, which, according to Kabbalistic doctrine, were necessary for the process of Creation.

A variety of values

SAADIAH GAON EMPHASIZED that no single value by itself is adequate. He[205] interprets the verse in Ecclesiastes "All is vanity, saith Koheleth, the vanity of vanities, all is vanity"[206] as denying that any one particular value alone suffices for a worthwhile life. The art of living consists in the attainment of the right mix of individual values. There is no simplistic principle that can be universally invoked to settle the conflicting claims of competing values. Various norms, ideals and values must be balanced against each other.

The Biblical account of Yiftah, the classic example of the ignorant leader, provides a telling illustration of the havoc created by reliance upon any single criterion. He had vowed that whoever or whatever would meet him first upon his victorious return from battle would be sacrificed to God. To his consternation, it turned out to be his own daughter. But Yiftah saw no way out. A vow was a vow! Its sanctity could not be violated. In his benightedness he did not realize that the sanctity of a vow had to be subordinated to the sanctity of life, and he tragically proceeded to destroy an innocent life.

While in some instances, as in the case of Yiftah, we have at our disposal a hierarchical structure of values (i.e., the sanctity of life overriding most other values), in many cases we have no guidelines whatsoever and are compelled to rely on our purely subjective intuitions to resolve agonizing moral dilemmas. This is one of the reasons why ethical decision-making is frequently fraught with many ambiguities.[207] With purely subjective intuitions playing such a decisive role in making value-judgments, it follows that in those cases where we cannot have recourse to clear-cut Halakhic rulings, a variety of moral positions may claim to represent *a,* not *the*, legitimate Jewish position.

The absence of uniformity in matters of belief as well as of conduct reflects the importance which Judaism places upon individuality. The Rabbis already contended that "no two prophets employed the same style."[208] Similarly, they emphasized the variety of ways in which God may be encountered. As Israel Baal Shem Tov noted, in our liturgy we do not simply invoke the God of our fathers, but add a reference to the God of Abraham, the God of Isaac, and the God of Jacob, in order to emphasize that each one of the Patriarchs had a unique, personal and special relationship with Him. For that matter, since each individual bears the Divine image in a unique way, human beings are irreplaceable. This is one of the reasons why "destroying one human life is tantamount to the destruction of the entire universe."[209]

There is an additional reason why Judaism views the diversity of approaches not as a source of weakness but of strength. Human beings cannot attain the absolute truth. It is only God, Who, according to the Talmud, bears the seal of Truth.[210] According to a well-known Midrash, God had to cast Truth from heaven to the ground in order to make possible the creation of man, who is utterly incapable of speaking the real truth.[211]

Since human opinions, at best, can only express partial glimpses but cannot possibly do justice to the requirements of the complete truth, discredited opinions may capture at least a grain of truth, which is ignored by the opinion in vogue. This is one of the reasons why minority opinions are recorded in the Talmud and their study is considered no less a fulfillment of a religious commandment than the study of majority opinions which are accepted as normative. Regardless of whether they are accepted or rejected, minority opinions nonetheless represent "the words of the Living God."[212]

That rejected opinions also add to the understanding of Torah can be seen from what at first blush appears as a most puzzling Rabbinic statement. The Mishnah asserts that "a controversy which is pursued for the sake of God will endure."[213] An illustration of such a controversy is the disagreement between the students of Hillel and those of Shammai.

Since Judaism extols peace and harmony and abhors controversy and strife, why should the perpetuation of a controversy be regarded as eminently desirable? The following explanation suggests itself. As long as the difference of opinion is not inspired by ulterior motives, *both* opinions express important elements of the truth. Obviously, in actual practice we can adopt only one of the two positions. But we ought to realize that each opinion reflects an aspect of the full truth.

Rav Joseph B. Soloveitchik utilizes the insight that no human opinion contains the full truth to explain why, for litigations, the Jewish legal system favors making compromises rather than offering strict legal rulings. He points out that no litigant has all the rights at his side, and therefore the ends of justice would best be served if both parties would agree to a settlement.[214]

Rav Kook went even further and took great pains to show that even wrong opinions contain a partial truth. While opposed to Christianity, he contended that its emergence was a necessary corrective. Since, at the time of the destruction of the second Temple, Judaism tended towards a one-sided legalism, Christianity went to the other extreme and provided a counter-balance by stressing the spirit and downplaying the importance of the law.[215] In a similar vein, Rav Kook contended that Marxism served as a valuable corrective to the excessive spiritualization of religion, which had neglected concern for the material well-being of society. Rav Kook's approach obviously reflects the Hegelian dialectic, in which the negation of both thesis and antithesis gives rise to the synthesis.

Individualism

MANY A READER WILL BE STARTLED by my emphasis upon subjectivity in matters of ideology and the significance attached to individuality and uniqueness, which runs counter to the widely held belief that Judaism is essentially communal and collectivistic in its orientation. Thus the eminent historian Salo Baron declared that insofar as Judaism is concerned "the nation overshadows the individual."[216] This characterization largely reflects the views of Ahad Ha'am, who had contended that the major difference between Judaism and Christianity is found in their respective attitudes towards the individual. Accordingly, whereas Christianity addresses itself to the individual, Judaism speaks to the collectivity. The Jewish conception of "the chosen people," represented "a Divine call to make its national life the embodiment of the highest form of religion and morality."[217]

Ahad Ha'am was convinced that, with its emphasis upon peoplehood and community, the ethnocentric orientation of Judaism left no room for concerns such as for the welfare or self-realization of the individual.

In the words of Ahad Ha'am:

"Judaism conceives its aim not as the salvation of the individual, but as the well-being and the perfection of the group, of the Jewish people, and ultimately of the human race." [218]

Because of his one-sided emphasis upon nationalism, Ahad Ha'am identifies with the position of the Sadducees who rejected the Pharisees' belief in personal immortality of the soul and in reward and punishment in the hereafter. He took it for granted that the belief in personal immortality arose only after "the Babylonian exile had put an end to the free national life of the Jews."

Professor Baron follows in his footsteps and maintains that Judaism sacrifices the individual on the altar of the collectivity. In his opinion, "Jewish ethics has remained, in essence, national rather than individual."[219] Moreover, he attributes the subjection to the Law, the hallmark of Jewish piety, to the national character of Judaism.

"The individual...must comply with it whether he understands its reasons or not. Its great aims transcend the individual, the Law has underlying motives which may remain hidden to him." [220]

This argument, however, is spurious. The fact that Halakhah has "supreme power over the individual"[221] by no means points to the insignificance of the individual. It is the very nature of any *legal* system to demand unconditional obedience to its provisions, irrespective of the personal feelings of its subjects. But this does not imply at all that the obedience to the Law is intended solely for the benefit of the nation as a whole. As a matter of fact, the Torah frequently appeals to individuals to observe the law for their own benefit. We therefore conclude that Judaism synthesizes the good of the individual with that of the collectivity.

JEWISH RESPONSIBILITY TO THE WORLD

FOR ALL THE EMPHASIS UPON the vital role which religion has played in the preservation of the Jewish people in the face of the vicissitudes of history, we cannot adopt Ahad Ha'am's approach and look upon Judaism primarily as a means to Jewish survival. Although Judaism views the Jewish people as God's chosen instrument for the realization of His Providential Design, the religious message of Judaism includes numerous universal concerns, which transcend the narrow bounds of a particular people. Judaism not only imposes upon Jews obligations towards non-Jews, but demands that the latter abide by the seven Noahide commandments.

Concern for the well-being of non-Jews was demonstrated by Abraham, who went so far as to risk incurring God's wrath by challenging His morality when he confronted God with the argument that the destruction of the inhabitants of Sodom contravened the dictates of justice.[222]

Jewish prophetic writings are replete with references to the historic destinies and missions of various nations. Especially telling is King Solomon's prayer offered at the dedication of the Temple in Jerusalem, in which he refers to the role which the Sanctuary ought to play in the lives of non-Jews[223] and which concludes with the hope that all the nations of the earth should know that "the Lord is God and no one else."[224]

This theme is echoed in the various references to the Messianic age, when, as mentioned before, not only the people of Israel will be restored to their pristine glory, but all the nations of the world will acknowledge the sovereignty of God. Then "from Zion shall go forth Torah and the word of the Lord from Jerusalem"[225] and all people will witness the end of exploitation, oppression and violence in an era of universal peace.

The universalistic thrust of Judaism by no means conflicts with the stress upon the uniqueness of the Jewish people. Even such an ardent nationalist as Rabbi Akiva, who declared that "Israelites are beloved because they are called God's children"[226] also maintained that not only Jews but every "human being is beloved because he/she was created in the image of God."[227]

Ways of peace

SOLICITUDE FOR ALL HUMAN BEINGS, regardless of their national or religious identity, is an important seminal principle in Jewish law. The Talmud mandates that "out of concern for the ways of peace, we are supposed to support non-Jewish poor...visit the non-Jewish sick...and bury the non-Jewish dead."[228] It is highly significant that, according to Maimonides, concern for the "ways of peace" is not due to considerations of expediency, but represents a response to the Divine commandment to "walk in the ways of God." In his interpretation, this passage represents an imperative to cultivate ethical dispositions and traits of character in emulation of His ethical attributes.[229]

The Rabbinic doctrine that, although non-Jews are exempt from most provisions of the Sinaitic legislation, they are subject to the "seven Noahide laws," is further evidence of the Torah's concern for the spiritual and moral welfare of non-Jews. Some Jewish authorities maintain that the "Noahide laws" encompass the entire range of ethical laws, because, in their opinion, the laws include whatever norms can be justified on the basis of "natural law."[230] A relatively popular Jewish view maintains that whatever law can be certified on purely rational grounds applies at all times and to all human beings.[231] Support for this view can be found in the fact that the prophet Ezekiel denounces the inhabitants of Sodom for their failure to attend to the needs of strangers,[232] in spite of the fact that the tradition nowhere includes philanthropy or the performance of acts of benevolence as duties ordained by Noahide laws.

In a similar vein, although the commandment to honor one's father or mother is not specifically mentioned among the seven Noahide laws, the Talmud[233] praises, as a paradigm of ethical conduct, the behavior of two non-Jews who displayed extraordinary sensitivity to the dignity of their parents. But a case can be made that just as the Ten Commandments can be interpreted as the basic principles from which all 613 commandments may be derived,[234] so the seven Noahide laws may be regarded as the seven basic categories under which all ethical commandments can be subsumed.

Regardless, whether we opt for a narrower or a broader construction of the seven Noahide laws, there can be no doubt that Judaism is vitally concerned with the sanctity and dignity as well as the property rights of all human beings. This, of course, does not imply that when it comes to helping others, there are no priorities. Since it is impossible to help or save everyone, hard choices must be made with respect to the allocation of priorities. According to the Jewish scale of values, which admittedly runs counter to the views of some liberal ethicists,[235] we have an obligation to help our own fellow members of the Jewish community, before we extend assistance to others. After all, even when we have to adjudicate between claims to assistance among our own people, we apply the principle "the poor of your own community take precedence over the poor of another community."[236]

Jewishness and Judaism

IN KEEPING WITH THIS ORIENTATION, classical Judaism would totally reject Hermann Cohen's contention that the ethical thrust of Judaism demands that the Jewish people forgo all aspirations for a Jewish State, because all national states are under moral obligation to give priority to the interests of their own citizens. In Cohen's opinion, such an attitude is incompatible with the ethical demands for universalizability, which calls for complete impartiality between competing claims.[237]

As against Cohen's utopian ethics, Judaism operates with a far more realistic approach, taking account of the requirements of human nature and prompting us to be more involved with our own children than those of others. These natural sentiments usually reinforce rather than conflict with ethical obligations. It makes perfect sense to argue that parenthood imposes special moral responsibilities to our children, over those we have towards others. This obligation is completely universalizable and applies to all parents. By the same token, the special bonds of solidarity and kinship between Jews provide ample moral justification for promoting the welfare of fellow Jews over those people further removed.

It therefore appears that the alleged conflict between universalism and particularism is a figment of the imagination. Within Judaism, both elements play a vital role. Any attempt to force Judaism into the strait jacket of either a universalistic ethics or a particularistic nationalism is bound to lead to a grotesque distortion of its true nature. Judaism and Jewishness have been joined together from the very beginning of our history and no amount of historic scholarship, theological sophistry or sociological jargon can rend them asunder.

There remains the challenge of finding the proper balance between Jewishness and Judaism – the two major ingredients of Jewish existence. Much depends upon historic contingencies. In his time, the prophet Jeremiah urged Jews to pray for the welfare of the city to which they were exiled.[238] But nowadays our moral responsibility for the common good is much greater in democratic societies, where Jews enjoy full civil rights and therefore bear responsibility for the policies pursued by their governments. There are no exact guidelines as to the proportion of efforts to be invested in general as compared with specific Jewish causes. But it is unconscionable for Jews to justify indifference to ecological concerns, for example, on the ground that these are not Jewish issues.

What is needed is a balancing act between advocacy of ethical concerns and the need to protect the self-interest of the Jewish community. Thus, during the war in Vietnam, many leading Orthodox spokesmen refused to voice criticism of the American involvement out of fear that such criticism would hurt the interests of the State of Israel. But Rav Aharon Soloveitchik was adamant in publicly condemning the immorality of the war. He compared the situation to the predicament of the prophet Jonah, who balked at carrying out his prophetic mission to persuade the inhabitants of Nineveh to reform their conduct. According to the Rabbinic Sages,[239] the reason for Jonah's failure to obey God's command was his love for the Jewish people. He was afraid that if his mission were to succeed, it would put his own people into a bad light. It would be said that whereas non-Jews heed the warning of the prophet, Jews are indifferent.[240] But, Rav Soloveitchik concluded, in spite of his noble intentions, Jonah sinned when he refused to carry out his mission, because we must not permit concern for Jewish self-interest to stand in the way of fulfilling our moral mandate.

In a similar vein, the State of Israel has a twofold mission. On the one hand, it must be concerned with its own security and, like any other nation, act in order to promote its own self-interest. On the other hand, without compromising its security, Israel must balance her need to serve as a bastion of Jewish survival with the requirements of Jewish moral principles which demand sensitivity to the dignity of every human being and responsiveness to the challenge to establish a truly just society.

INTEGRATING OPPOSING VALUES INTO THE SERVICE OF GOD

OUR DISCUSSION OF THE NEED to reconcile the demands of universalism with those of particularism, as well as of the requirement to synthesize polar values, point to the complex structure of religious faith. Contrary to popular belief, religion does not offer easy solutions to difficult problems. It has no ready-made answers to perplexing questions. At times, it even creates problems which do not exist for the non-believer. Thus, for example, the so-called problem of evil arises only for the theist, whereas the prevalence of pain and suffering poses no difficulties for the naturalist.

What religious faith provides us with is the challenge to integrate our personalities in keeping with the ideal of *Imitatio Dei*. As mentioned previously, belief in the absolute unity of God prods us towards the unification of our selves by channeling all our drives, appetites and personality resources to His service.[241] No single mood, emotion or attitude, be it love, faith or self-surrender can claim a monopoly in our religious economy. Variety is the order of the day. According to the Talmud, the Biblical verse "In all thy ways thou shalt acknowledge Him"[242] best sums up the sweeping range over which Jewish piety extends.²⁴³ There are innumerable avenues of service to God; every psychological drive can be harnessed towards this goal.

As we have noted previously, we are mandated not only to love God but also to fear Him. During the "Days of Awe" we unabashedly beseech God to "place Thy fear upon us." We pray not for the conquest of fear, but for its proper use.

Judaism maintains that every attitude can be hallowed (not merely sublimated) in the service of God. In this scheme, there is room for self-regarding as well as for altruistic motives, for the Freudian libido as well as the death-instinct, for self-realization as well as self-surrender. All the elements of our psychological make-up can be channeled into the service of God.

Human nature and the ideal of selfless service

EVEN A PURELY SELF-CENTERED orientation can be utilized in the service of sublime ideals. Thus, when donors, inspired by the belief that "Charity is the salt [the preservative] of money" are motivated exclusively by concern for their own well-being, their conduct is approved by the Talmud.²⁴⁴

This does not mean that motives are irrelevant. According to Jewish tradition, whenever an act of charity is motivated by haughtiness, arrogance, or the desire to humiliate others, it becomes a spiritual liability. Nietzsche was by no means the first to discover that at times charity springs from resentment rather than love.²⁴⁵ The Talmudic Sages were astute enough psychologists to recognize that the veneer of charity frequently covers base emotions.

Yet, insofar as the Rabbinic position is concerned, nothing but what transpires at the *conscious* level is relevant to the evaluation of the worthwhileness of charity. Charitable giving is condemned only when it serves as a means to give vent to haughtiness or arrogance, e.g., when a philanthropist relishes his feelings of superiority over his "inferior" fellow human being who depends upon sustenance provided by a benefactor. Thus, it is only when philanthropy represents a deliberate act of self-aggrandizement rather than a manifestation of loving-kindness that it is condemned.[246] But the Rabbis would part company with Nietzsche when charity arises out of a *sublimated* sense of resentment. What takes place on the subconscious level cannot affect the merits of an act. The transformation of an undesirable psychological trait into a wholesome one would be regarded as a spiritual triumph of the highest order. We fulfill our religious task to the extent that we succeed in sublimating unbecoming drives and desires and harness them into the service of the Creator.

Owing to the intrinsic limitations besetting human nature, the ideal can never be fully realized. The Rabbis, therefore, encouraged the performance of good deeds, even if prompted by ulterior motives.[247] This realistic approach was justified on the ground that, eventually, the habit of performing good deeds may succeed in transforming our character so that we may reach a level of piety where the good deed is inspired only by the desire to serve God.[248]

Many scholars maintain that such totally disinterested service is a realistic possibility. Rabbi Chaim of Volozin, however, scales down what he considers to be extravagant claims for the efficacy of this approach. What emerges is a far less flattering picture of the human potential for completely selfless service. He anticipates no miracle cure for selfishness or egocenteredness. All he hopes for is that the repeated performance of good deeds will eventually lead to some refinement of our character so that at least the desire to serve God will also be *one* among many motives.[249] Reinhold Niebuhr and other neo-orthodox Christian theologians may be completely right when they call attention to the selfishness that mars so much of what masquerades as selfless love. But Judaism does not suffer from perfectionist pretensions. Granted that even our noblest sentiments and finest actions are tainted by residual traces of selfishness, resentment, or even outright hostility, we still are not justified in disparaging the worthwhileness of moral efforts. In the Jewish scheme, the recognition of our imperfections leads, not to a Pauline obsession with original sin, but to a design for the "ultimate sanctification" of all the elements comprising our biological and psychological make-up. We do not end up with a vicious perfectionism where the damned and doomed individual depends for Redemption from sinfulness upon a gratuitous act of grace bestowed upon those who possess "faith." Instead, we emphasize moral responsibility, which manifests itself in a never-ending quest for self-perfection.

The ultimate objective of this incessant striving mirrors the structure of Jewish piety, with its focus upon ethical and psychological pluralism. We do not seek the exclusive cultivation of any one drive or, for that matter, even a limited set of "ideal" attitudes and the concomitant repression of other "lower" drives. Our pattern for the unification of the personality is woven out of a variety of strands. We seek not the reduction of our staggering psychological riches, but their integration into a unifying vision and ideal.

Halakhic guidance

THE HALAKHIC SYSTEM, too, manages to incorporate divergent and even antithetical values. This is made possible by the ingenious use of a system of checks and balances, preventing any one norm or value from completely dominating the entire domain. Thus, the Halakhah succeeds in combining an emphasis upon the moral law with an awareness that all moral principles must be handled with care, lest their rigorous application, without counter-balancing safeguards, yield a harvest of paradoxes and absurdities.

The road of morality may be fraught with grave perils. The abyss of ethical ambiguity gapes on both sides. Yet, the Jew traverses the narrow bridge over the abyss, grasping the guiding rail provided by the checks and balances in the Halakhic system.

Proceeding under halakhic guidance, we can safely uphold the infinite worth and dignity of the human individual without risking self-idolization. Since the Halakhah protects us from confusing freedom with autonomy, there is no danger that we may become so intoxicated with the ideal of self-emancipation as to follow Kant in branding obedience to laws out of respect for Divine authority, as unworthy of free moral creatures. For the

Halakhah, the road to freedom does not lead over the repudiation of all heteronomous ethics. On the contrary, it involves the union of self-surrender with self-emancipation.

But for all the importance assigned to humble surrender to God, Judaism has no room for the debunking of reason that is so characteristic of modern existentialism. The kind of self-surrender advocated by Halakhah does not reduce human beings to lowly creatures cringing in the dust of moral unworthiness and intellectual insignificance. Since the Halakhah must be interpreted in conformity with the "ways of peace" and the "ways of pleasantness," the Halakhic approach is by no means so one-sided, narrow and formalistic as to banish from its sphere everything but blind submission to the rules of the Law.

In addition to mandating such humanistic values as justice, truth and peace, the Halakhah also contains more general commandments such as "thou shalt do what is right and good," "ye shall be holy," or "thou shalt walk in His ways," which enjoin the cultivation of ethical sensibilities. In quest of such beckoning ideals, human beings must *develop* their admittedly limited moral and intellectual capacities – not blunt them as an expression of "ontological despair."

THE SABBATH: A MODEL OF INTEGRATION

IF, AS GLADSTONE PUT IT, one picture is worth a thousand arguments, it would be extremely useful to adduce a specific example to illustrate how one fundamental Jewish practice incorporates polar values. A most telling illustration will be provided by an analysis of the Sabbath, an institution which is widely regarded as the quintessence of Judaism.[250]

A well-known Midrash suggests that the Sabbath cannot be accounted for in terms of any one single idea but involves a synthesis of different values.

> *"Everything associated with the Sabbath displays duality: a double portion of the Omer (of Mannah), double sacrifices, double penalties, double rewards, double prohibitions, and the Sabbath Psalm is [introduced by] a twofold term."*[251]

The two versions of the Decalogue

THAT DUALITY PLAYS A DECISIVE role in the Sabbath is emphasized in a frequently quoted comment on the Decalogue. It notes that while Exodus and Deuteronomy present us with different formulations of the fourth Commandment, they both were simultaneously pronounced at Sinai.[252]

Upon closer inspection we find that there are enormous differences between these two versions of the observance of the Sabbath. In Exodus, the Sabbath revolves exclusively around the creation theme. We are enjoined to refrain from work on the seventh day of the week for, by doing so, we acknowledge God as the Creator of the universe. We are reminded that the world does not belong to us, but to God. Hence, human activity must conform to the pattern established by God who stopped the process of Creation on the Sabbath.

In this thoroughly theocentric formulation, there is no mention of any benefits accruing to humanity. "The seventh day is a Sabbath for the Lord your God." A person's right to engage in creative activity is subject to the constraints imposed by the Author and Owner of the universe. Thus in this version of the Decalogue the accent is placed upon absolute surrender to God. Human beings are cut down to size, lest we worship our own powers and incur the sin of self-deification. The Bible finds it necessary to admonish us against the danger of thinking "my power and the might of my hand has secured for me all this wealth.[253] Instead, we should bear in mind that "the Lord, thy God, gives you the power to create wealth."[254]

An entirely different conception emerges in the formulation of the Decalogue in Deuteronomy. In addition to the creation theme, the fourth commandment includes a reference to the Exodus from Egypt and dwells upon the benefits accruing to humanity from the Sabbath as a day of universal liberation and rest. Even animals are entitled to a day of rest. This humanistic motif is further expanded in the Book of Isaiah, where the proclamation of the Sabbath as a day of delight is mandated.[255] In keeping with this approach, the Tannaim emphasized that the observance of the Sabbath is not merely the fulfillment of a commandment but should be hailed as a special and unique gift bestowed upon Israel by the Almighty.[256]

It must, however, be emphasized that, contrary to Hermann Cohen and Erich Fromm, "social hygiene" functions such as providing rest and relief from drudgery, and restoring dignity to all segments of society, represent merely secondary considerations. It is because the Sabbath serves as the sign between God and Israel that He is the Creator of Heaven and earth, that the desecration of the Sabbath amounts not merely to an act of disobedience, but is construed as an outright denial of one of the most pivotal tenets of Judaism – the affirmation of God as the Creator of the universe.

Were the advancement of human welfare through securing rest from toil and labor for even the lowliest member of society, and even animals, the main objective of the Sabbath, it would hardly make sense for Jewish law to contain provisions that only activities performed with design and purpose fall under the category of Biblically prohibited work. In the Halakhic framework, the amount of effort involved in any activity is totally irrelevant to the determination of whether the activity in question constitutes Biblically forbidden *melekhet machshevet* (activity performed with design and purpose in the normal fashion).

The Halakhic definition of *melakhah* as purposeful work, rather than as toil and labor, points to the specifically religious dimension of the Sabbath, which transcends such ethical considerations as social utility or mental health benefits. If Isaiah[257] and Nehemiah[258] single out the observance of the Sabbath as the hallmark of Biblical faith, it was because they saw in the Sabbath the crystallization of the most fundamental tenets of Judaism.

According to Maimonides, the original Divine legislation promulgated at Marah, as described in Exodus 15:28, dealt only with the Sabbath and with civil law; the various other ritual laws which were subsequently enacted at Sinai were only deemed necessary because of historic contingencies prevailing at that time. Small wonder, then, that in the words of I. Grunfeld, the "Sabbath epitomizes the whole of Judaism." It appears, therefore, that the prohibition against work on the Sabbath is primarily intended to impress upon us that since the universe was created by God and belongs to Him, we must remember that we are merely creatures of God and must employ our powers of creativity strictly within the parameters permitted by Him.

The Sabbath: A Model Of Integration

Partners with God

TO BE SURE, HUMAN CREATIVITY and the exercise of dominion over nature are not merely condoned but endorsed by Judaism, which seeks to make human beings into "partners with God in the process of Creation."[259] This orientation is totally opposed to the spirit of the Promethean myth, which condemned human creativity as an act of defiance of the heavenly powers. The Biblical account of the building of the Tower of Babel was never interpreted in Judaism as a condemnation of human initiative. In the view of the Sages, Divine displeasure was provoked, not because human creativity constituted an infringement upon Divine prerogatives, but because the building of the tower was intended as a declaration of war against the heavenly powers.

There is really no basis whatsoever for Eric Fromm's contention that the prohibition against work on the Sabbath aims at the reconciliation of humanity with nature and the ensuing restoration of the peace that has been disturbed by human efforts to assert dominion over nature.[260] However appealing this explanation may be to an age that is becoming increasingly sensitivized to ecological issues, the religious tradition cannot be invoked to justify such anti-technological bias. Even under the idyllic conditions prevailing in the Garden of Eden, so a Midrash informs us, it was necessary for man to engage in work and to put his stamp on nature. God placed Adam into the garden "to tend and to guard it."[261]

In the light of these considerations, we reject Fromm's claim that the Sabbath is intended as a protest against human interference with nature. There is no basis for his thesis that reconciliation with nature, as evidenced by the cessation of human constructive activities, constitutes an integral part of the Messianic ideal of perfect *shalom* – the ultimate peace of which the Sabbath is a precursor.

It therefore seems much more likely that the stringent prohibitions against working on the Sabbath have nothing to do with negative attitudes towards the manipulation or control of nature, but are grounded in the realization that our creativity frequently exposes us to debilitating spiritual hazards. It is one thing to endorse human creativity as the fulfillment of a God-given mandate to exercise dominion over the world and to harness the forces of nature to satisfy human needs, and another to become oblivious to the enormous dangers which our technological triumphs pose to our spiritual health. As we have so painfully discovered in our age of secularization and desacralization, we are prone to become so intoxicated with our success in subduing nature that we succumb to arrogant self-deification and forget that the entire universe, including our own creative capacities, is not a self-contained cosmos but a Divine creation, which is totally dependent upon Him. Had we taken this message to heart, we might have avoided the ecological crisis of our age, which resulted from one-sided preoccupation with technological progress, irrespective of all social consequences.

The regularity and order governing the realm of nature tend to obscure the Divine source of all existence. It is for this reason that precisely on the Sabbath, the day when, according to the Biblical account, the universe began to function in accordance with the laws of nature, it is incumbent upon us to acknowledge God as the Owner and Master of the universe.

By abstaining from productive activities on the day on which the Creator "stopped" His work of creation, we affirm that what appears to the secular mind as purely natural processes are in actuality manifestations of the Divine. Thus, the Sabbath reveals what nature conceals. We are challenged to penetrate beneath the surface, to the core of reality, so that we may apprehend that the universe is not a self-contained cosmos, but is created and sustained in its being by the Divine Creator – the source of all reality.

Unfortunately, some liberal Jewish thinkers completely ignore the theocentric formulation of Exodus, which omits any reference to the psychological and social benefits which render the Sabbath such a boon to humanity.

Hermann Cohen and Eric Fromm, who dismiss obedience to heteronomous norms as devoid of all ethical worth, focus exclusively on the Deuteronomy version of the fourth Commandment, which adds to the Creation theme other humanistic elements such as liberation and rest to be enjoyed by all creatures. They attempt to attribute the discrepancies to the contrast between the "mythological" version of Exodus and the "ethical" account in Deuteronomy, because they dogmatically insist that Judaism be forced into a Procrustean bed of humanistic categories. Actually, the added references in Deuteronomy to social benefits do not in any manner detract from the theocentric aspects mandating total surrender to the Creator and Master of the universe. It is precisely in the version in which the humanistic elements are introduced that the Torah stresses the observance of the Sabbath as a Divine imperative.

It is therefore more appropriate to look upon the contrast between the two versions of the Decalogue as a dialectical tension between two integral components, rather than an unbridgeable gap. As opposed to Feuerbach and Marx, Jews maintain that unconditional submission to God is not the source of self-alienation. Far from diminishing the significance of human existence, it adds an extra dimension of meaning and purpose and enables us to experience true dignity and freedom. Observance of the Sabbath makes us aware that our ontological status depends not on what we make but on what we are. People are bearers of the Divine image. Regardless of their social or economic status, they must be accorded the dignity due to creatures who are endowed with infinite, spiritual value. Needless to say, they must not be "thingified" or reduced to self-alienated commodities or tools of production. The Sabbath teaches us the vital ethical axiom that a person's worth is not measured in terms of social utility, but derives from the intrinsic sanctity of the human personality.

The paradox of the Sabbath

IT MAY STRIKE US AS paradoxical that the observance of the Sabbath, which is designed to remind us that we are mere creatures who may exercise their creative powers only within the parameters established by God, simultaneously enhances our sense of dignity by providing us with a day of universal rest and liberation. But since the Sabbath represents the quintessence of all of Judaism, it is not surprising that we find in it the reflection of the fundamental Jewish conviction that humans achieve true dignity and inner freedom solely through submission to the will of God. Viewed from the perspective of Judaism, our efforts to utilize technology in the quest for the improvement of the human condition arises not from the desire to reduce our dependence upon God, but rather from the resolve to fulfill our ethico-religious duty to imitate the Divine Creator as much as humanly possible for us. The Sabbath directs us toward a proper balance between the conflicting requirements of a human self which is aware of its connection with its transcendent source. In fact, the very first mention of holiness in the entire Bible is with reference to the Sabbath. The opportunity for physical rest on the Sabbath should be utilized for spiritual growth, resulting in all-out efforts to respond to the dynamic ideal of holiness, which constantly beckons us towards ever greater heights of moral perfection in the quest for the imitation of God's moral attributes.

The Sabbath is described in the liturgy as a "day of rest and of holiness." Rabbi A. I. Kook pointed out that these two characterizations seem to be contradictory. For holiness is a dynamic rather than a static property, which conflicts with the objective of providing a day of rest.[262] The paradox, however, can easily be resolved. The Sabbath is not a day of inactivity. On the contrary, it is a summons to holiness through activities designed to develop a higher level of spirituality.

Since the Sabbath represents the fusion of the ritualistic and ethical strands of Judaism, of self-realization as well as of self-surrender, it is readily understandable that Isaiah assured us that the proper observance of the Sabbath will enable us to "find delight in the Lord's goodness."[263] Our Sages went even further and characterized the Sabbath "as a foretaste of the world-to-come."[264]

THE QUEST FOR GOD AND THE EMULATION OF HIS ETHICAL ATTRIBUTES

IN THE PRECEDING CHAPTER WE EMPHASIZED the strong linkage between ritualistic and ethical elements, which form a seamless whole in Judaism. Significantly, the prophet Isaiah[265] first went to great lengths to denounce those who failed to realize that ethical conduct was a prerequisite to any kind of closeness to God. It was only afterwards that he extolled experiencing the Sabbath as a delight, as a prelude to reaching the greatest height of spiritual joy.

On the other hand, some Jewish authorities view moral conduct primarily as a necessary condition for the survival of society, but not as an integral feature of piety itself. Yehudah HaLevi maintained that the prophets harped so much upon the importance of ethical laws, not because of their intrinsic religious significance, but because no society can endure when the moral law is flouted. Even a gang of robbers cannot function without an internal moral code.[266] On the other hand, he said, the cultivation of our *religious* potential depended primarily upon the observance of ritual laws.[267]

We encounter an entirely different approach in Maimonides. To begin with, he contended that all Divine laws have one of three functions: They 1) convey basic religious truths, 2) enhance the physical or moral/spiritual well-being of individuals, or 3) promote the collective welfare of society.[268] In the concluding chapter of the *Guide*, Maimonides views the emulation of Divine moral attributes as the highest level of religious perfection, despite his insistence upon the primacy of intellectual development.

In this context, it is important to remember that, in Judaism, moral requirements are not just demands made upon us by reason or nature, but represent Divine commands. Even when, as in supererogatory conduct (going beyond minimal legal or moral requirements), specific acts are not explicitly mandated by God, they are recommended as an effort to come closer to the Divinely ordained religious ideal of "emulating God's ways." In my *Ethics of Responsibility*, I have adduced evidence to show that some provisions of Jewish ethics cannot possibly be accounted for in terms of social utility, but make sense only within a theocentric framework.[269]

Striving to imitate God

IN HIS ESSAY *UVIKASHTEM*,[270] Rav Soloveitchik explains why the striving for moral perfection plays such a pre-eminent role in Judaism. Initially, once we become aware that God is completely beyond our reach, we settle for mere obedience to His commandments. At this stage, the commandments represent completely heteronomous laws. But after this phase of religious development, it dawns upon us that when we strive to imitate God's moral attributes, we proceed to a higher level of closeness to God as we appropriate, however imperfectly, some of His attributes. Our response to His commandments relating to ethical conduct will no longer be in the category of obedience to heteronomously dictated laws, but will reflect the promptings of a theonomous conscience, which has internalized some of His commandments.

In his widely quoted *Netivot Olam*, Rav Judah ben Bezalel Loew pointed out that one who merely obeys a Divine commandment cannot be called "one who walks in the ways of God." One merits this honorific designation only by performance of supererogatory acts of loving kindness.

"[Only] he who walks by himself and acts by himself out of his own will and understanding...can be called "one who walks in the ways of God."[271]

In his view, when one makes a charitable contribution, one is merely following an explicit rule of the Torah which mandates that we open our hands to the poor. But what constitutes a *benevolent* action is not so clearly defined. To fulfill the commandment of acting benevolently we must utilize our own moral perception as to the needs of particular individuals.[272] It is no longer a matter of obeying clear-cut moral rules. A certain degree of wisdom is indispensable to attaining the kind of moral insight and vision necessary for this level of ethical conduct. As Maimonides put it in his Commentary on the Mishnah, only the lower level of ethical conduct is within reach of individuals who are lacking intellectual virtues.[273] This explains why, according to Rav Loew, the higher level of piety can be reached only when a meritorious action ceases to be performed solely as a duty imposed by Divine command, but is motivated by an agent's awareness of its desirability.[274]

One may be tempted to raise the question as to the legitimacy of Rav Loew's position, especially since the Talmud regards religious acts as more significant when they are responses to God's command rather than when they represent voluntarily assumed obligations.[275] For this reason, writing in his *Arukh Hashulchan*, Rav Yechiel Mikhal Epstein argues that even such a universally accepted practice as honoring one's parents should be engaged in, not only for humanistic ethical reasons, but should be motivated by the desire to comply with a Divine imperative.[276].

There is, however, a significant precedent for the distinction made by Rav Loew. Maimonides, too, contended that ethical laws ideally should be obeyed without any inner struggle because we have reached a stage where our own inclinations completely coincide with them. But this prescription does not apply to ritual laws.

On the contrary, since "the reward is proportionate to the effort,"[277] performing them is regarded as more meritorious when it involves the suppression of contrary personal inclinations.[278]

It has been claimed, erroneously, that in making this distinction, Maimonides was influenced by Greek philosophy, especially its doctrine of virtue. On the contrary, his rationale is based upon his highly original and creative interpretation of Jewish law. He viewed the commandment "thou shalt walk in His ways" as the prooftext for the obligation to cultivate moral dispositions.[279] He felt that this commandment has not been properly fulfilled as long as one's conformity to ethical requirements is not effortless but involves a struggle against contrary inclinations. When one obeys an ethical law merely out of a sense of obedience to God, one has not acquired a virtuous personality and one remains religiously defective. Maimonides even states that repentance is required not only for evil deeds, but even for the mere possession of bad traits of character.[280] Since, with respect to ritual laws, there is no corresponding requirement of effortless obedience, compliance with these laws become actually more meritorious in proportion to the difficulties endured in carrying them out.

Ethical and ritual obligations

IT IS IMPORTANT TO NOTE that the recommendation to engage in supererogatory conduct is mandated only with respect to ethical requirements but does not extend to the realm of ritual law. Of course, with respect to the observance of the Law itself there is no distinction between ethical and ritual obligations. Scrupulous adherence even to the minutiae of ritual law is demanded. But once it is clearly established that a certain procedure unquestionably satisfies Halakhic ritual requirements, it no longer makes sense to look for additional stringencies.

There is good reason for this distinction. Ritual law involves simply submission to Divine authority. Moral conduct, as Rav Soloveitchik was wont to emphasize, ultimately revolves around the religious norm of Imitatio Dei. With respect to this requirement Maimonides emphasizes that Divine moral perfection is an ideal that is forever beyond our reach. But each individual is supposed to strive to approximate it "according to one's capacity."[281]

I am inclined to look upon what the Torah says about justice as a paradigm for all ethical values. Many commentators are puzzled why the Torah (Deuteronomy 16:20) repeats the word 'justice' in the verse "Justice, justice shalt thou pursue." In my opinion, the repetition is designed to make us realize that the requirements of justice are never fully met. What was just in a feudal society, may not meet the standards of justice in a modern democratic society. Similarly, although at one time nobody thought that social justice mandates providing health care for the needy, nowadays many believe that the unavailability of health care to any segment of the population is a denial of human rights and constitutes injustice. Since justice is a dynamic conception, we must forever be engaged in the *pursuit* of justice by continuous re-examination of our conduct and institutions in quest of this forever elusive ideal.

This ought to be our model for all moral values. Responding to the Biblical mandate "and thou shalt walk in His ways,"[282] we must continuously strive to develop our spiritual potential so that we may come nearer to the ever elusive ideal of imitating God's ethical perfection. In the words of the Rabbinic Sages, "It is not up to us to finish the task; but we are not free to give it up."[283]

There is an ancient Midrash,[284] which seems to support our thesis that religious faith calls for never-ending efforts to come ever closer to God through striving for moral perfection. Commenting on Psalm 100:3, in which the Hebrew term *velo* which is spelled with the letter *aleph* (meaning: *and not*) but is read as if it were spelled with a *vav* (meaning: *His*), two alternate interpretations are offered. Rav Yehudah explains its meaning in conformity with the *Ketiv* (the written version). Accordingly, the verse should be rendered as "Know ye that the Lord is God; it is He Who hath made us and *not we* ourselves." But Rav Aha followed the *Keri* (the Masoretic instructions for reading the text) and rendered the second part of the sentence as "it is He Who hath made us and we *are His*," emphasizing that our awareness "that God hath made us" inspires us to "to perfect our souls towards Him." In other words, our monotheistic faith amounts to not merely the affirmation of a metaphysical belief, but mandates incessant striving towards ever higher levels of ethical perfection.

We thus note that genuine true faith is not "an opiate" which induces smugness, equanimity and serenity. The Talmud ridicules self-righteous individuals who boast that they have fully discharged all their religious obligations.[285] On the contrary, as we previously indicated, faith possesses a dynamic quality, which does not permit us to be satisfied with our spiritual achievements but propels us to search for ever higher levels of perfection. This is why the Rabbinic sages maintained that a perpetual state of spiritual restlessness is the hallmark of the truly religious personality, and declared that "Torah scholars have no rest either in this world or in the next, because they go from strength to strength."[286]

I often think of the impact made upon me by a portrait of the famous psychologist and philosopher, William James. What struck me was that the artist, instead of affixing his signature, inscribed the words, "Not quite!" – a phrase intended to characterize the artist's inability to produce a perfect portrayal of his subject.

"Not quite" also describes our efforts to attain justice, truth and other moral and religious ideals. All we can do is strive to come ever closer to them, while realizing that we can never fully attain them.

THE NEVER-ENDING SEARCH

AS WE REACH THE CONCLUSION of this book, it becomes increasingly evident that religious faith cannot be obtained at one particular moment and subsequently stored away for future use. Faith cannot be preserved; it must forever be cultivated and developed.

Religious faith involves a perpetual quest. It does not purport to offer ready-made answers to all questions. As we noted in our discussion of the problem of evil, faith may even give rise to agonizing problems. What distinguishes religious faith is not so much the answers it provides, as the nature of the questions it asks in various situations, especially, "What does God demand of us?" Religious belief challenges us to steadfastly confirm our faith as we face all of life's experiences.

Rabbi Joseph B. Soloveitchik pointed out that, unfortunately, most people look upon the twenty-third Psalm, with its idyllic portrayal of green pastures and still waters, as the very essence of religious faith. In his opinion, it is the image of Jacob wrestling with the angel which does more justice to the true nature of genuine faith. Although wounded in the struggle and limping as a result of the encounter, Jacob emerges from it with a new honorific name, Israel, which is conferred upon him in recognition of his elevation to a higher spiritual status.

Constant search for God provides the meaning of life for

pious individuals. It is the never-ending search for God which constitutes the hallmark of the genuinely pious and endows their existence with meaning. As the Psalmist declared, "Let the heart of them rejoice that seek God."[287] According to a classical Chassidic insight, in most areas, acts of searching yield satisfaction only when they achieve desirable results. But the search for God is different. Here the *act* of *seeking* itself constitutes the source of satisfaction.

The human task is to persevere in the search and attempt to relate the totality of our experiences to our awareness of God. This is why Maimonides, in his exposition of the first commandment of the Decalogue[288] includes the requirement to relate all events and phenomena of our natural world to God.

Cultivation of such a faith is not a one-time achievement, but an on-going task. To see how wrong Alfred Kazin was when, in his *Walker in the City,* he observed that for Jews "God is our oldest habit,"[289] we need but recall a striking Rabbinic comment on the verse, "They are new every morning,"[290] in which the Talmud[291] remarks that faith must never be permitted to become stale. It must always be in the process of being constantly renewed and revitalized. What Hegel said about truth, "Truth is not a minted coin that can be handed over and accepted as a finished product,"[292] should be applied to religious faith.

Faith must never remain merely a matter of fealty to tradition, nor cherished as an heirloom of the past. Because genuine faith must always be in the making, we open our prayers with an invocation addressed to "our God and God of our fathers." Similarly, after the miraculous rescue of the Israelites at the Red Sea, they proclaimed "This is my God and I shall glorify Him," and only afterwards continued with "the God of my father, and shall exalt Him."[293]

Our journey of faith must begin with our own personal encounter with *our* God. Only then can the God of our fathers become relevant to us. But the cultivation of such a faith requires more than a sudden leap. It can be brought about only through an arduous, gradual ascent to the Mountain of the Lord, which requires the all-out mobilization of our intellectual resources in the constant search for the traces He left in His creation.

SOURCES AND BIBLIOGRAPHY

[1] William James, *The Will to Believe and other Essays in Popular Philosophy*, edited by Frederick H. Burkhardt, Cambridge, Harvard University Press, 1979.

[2] Prayerbook, morning service.

[3] B.T. (Babylonian Talmud) Shabbat 58a.

[4] Leo Strauss, *Natural Right and History*, The University of Chicago Press, Chicago, 1953, p.248.

[5] *The Holy Scriptures*, Jewish Publication Society, Philadelphia, 1955, Leviticus, 19:10.

[6] For a justification of the legitimacy of advocating public policy on the basis of religious reasons see Jeff Jordan's "Religious Reasons and Public Reasons," *Public Affairs Quarterly*, 11, 3, July 1997, pp.245-254.

[7] I am indebted to the works of communitarians such as Charles Taylor, Alister McIntyre and Michael Sandel for calling my attention to the shortcomings of the atomistic self.

[8] Leviticus 19:18.

[9] J.T. (Jerusalem Talmud) Nedarim 9:4. This conception underlies Moses Cordovaro's approach in his *Tomer Devorah*, where his ethical views reflect the belief in the underlying unity of mankind.

[10] Bereshit Rabbah, 39:3.

[11] B.T. Bava Metzia, 62a.

[12] Soren Kierkegaard, *Sickness unto Death*, quoted in W.H. Auden. *The Living Thoughts of Kierkegaard,* Bloomington, Indiana University Press, 1966, p.151.

[13] Genesis, 4:12.

[14] Isaiah, 57:20-21.

[15] Nachmanides, Torah Commentary on Genesis 4:17.

[16] Deuteronomy 30:1-6.

[17] B.T. Megilah 17b.

[18] Isaiah 57-21.

[19] Jonah 1:3.

[20] Leviticus 16:30.

[21] Mishna Yoma 8:9.

[22] Abraham Isaac Kook, *The Lights of Penitence*, translated by Ben Zion Bokser, Paulist Press, New York,1978, Chapter VI, p.56.

[23] Pinchas Peli, *Soloveitchik On Repentance: The Thought and Oral Discourses Of Rabbi Joseph B. Soloveitchik*, Ramsey, Paulist Press, 1984, p.90.

[24] Genesis 2:18.

[25] See Karl Jaspers, Gabriel Marcel, Martin Buber and R.Joseph B. Soloveitchik. Significantly, the atheistic existentialist Jean Paul Sartre categorically rules out the possibility of developing a proper sense of community, because all interpersonal relations are based upon conflict.

[26] G.E.M. Anscombe, "Modern Moral Philosophy," in *Journal of Philosophical Studies*, 33, 1958, pp.13-14.

[27] Robert Nozick, *Philosophical Explanations*, Cambridge: Harvard University Press, 1981, p.401 ff.

[28] Micah 6:8.

[29] Walter S. Wurzburger, *Ethics of Responsibility*, Philadelphia, Jewish Publication Society of America, 1994.

[30] Psalms 16:8.

[31] Psalms 111:10. Cf. also Proverbs 1:7.

[32] Maimonides, *Guide for the Perpexed* III, 51-54.

[33] Leviticus 19:19.

[34] Emil L. Fackenheim, "Abraham and the Kantians" in *Encounters Between Judaism and Modern Philosophy*, New York, Jason Aronson, 1994, pp.51-53.

[35] Cf. Emil L.Fackenheim, *Ibid*.

[36] A considerable part of this chapter is based upon my article "Orthodox Judaism and Human Purpose" in *Religion and Human Purpose*, W. Horosz and T. Clements, (eds.) Martin J. Nijhoff, Dortrecht, 1986, reprinted by permission of Kluwer Academic Publishers.

[37] This benediction reflects the position of the conclusion of *Perek*

Kinyan Torah (often cited as Avot 6), which adduces Scriptural support from Isaiah 43:7.

[38] Maimonides, *Guide for the Perplexed*, III,15.

[39] I have dealt with this issue in my essay, "Orthodox Judaism and Human Purpose," in *Religion and Human Purpose*, edited by William Horocz and T. Clements, Dortrecht, Martin Nijhoff Publishers, 1986, pp.105-122.

[40] Saadiah, *Book of Beliefs and Opinions*, Chapter 10.

[41] Avot 4:17.

[42] Genesis 1.

[43] *Ibid*. 1:26.

[44] See my essay, "The Centrality of Creativity in the Thought of Rabbi Joseph B. Soloveitchik," *Tradition*, 30:4, 1996, pp.219-228.

[45] Deuteronomy 28:10.

[46] See my *Tradition* article, *op. cit.* and my "*Imitatio Dei* in the Philosophy of Rabbi Joseph B. Soloveitchik" in *Hazon Nachum*, edited by Yaakov Elman and Jeffrey S. Gurock, New York, Yeshiva University Press, 1997, pp.557-575.

[47] Exodus 21:25.

[48] B.T. Bava Kama 83b-84a.

[49] B.T. Gittin 60b.

[50] B.T. Bava Metzia 59b.

[51] Maimonides, Code. Hilkhot Yesodei Hatorah, 9:4.

Sources And Bibliography

[52]B.T. Megillah 29a; J.T. Taanit 1:1.

[53]B.T. Sotah 31a.

[54]B.T. Berakhot 7b.

[55]Avot 1:3.

[56]Maimonides, Code, Hilkhot Teshuvah, 10:1.

[57]Mishnah Berakhot 2:2.

[58]Deuteronony 6:5.

[59]B.T. Berakhot 61b.

[60]Daily Prayerbook.

[61]B.T. Berakhot 12a.

[62]Rashi Commentary to Deuteronomy 6:4.

[63]Zechariah 14:9.

[64]Isaiah 11:9.

[65]B.T. Berakhot 63a.

[66]Proverbs 3:6.

[67]Maimonides, Code, Hilkhot Deot, 3:3.

[68]Avot 2:12.

[69]Rav Soloveitchik referred to this in many of his lectures.

[70]Exodus 20:2.

[71]B.T. Bava Metzia 10a.

[72] Perek Kinyan Torah (Avot) 6:2.

[73] B.T. Kiddushin 32b.

[74] Psalms 1:2.

[75] See especially the Torah commentary of Nachmanides *ad locum*.

[76] Genesis Rabbah 17:2. Cf. also B.T. Yevamot 63a.

[77] Avot 2:4.

[78] Maimonides, Code, Hilkhot Teshuvah 10:3.

[79] *Ibid*, 1:1. See also Peli, *op. cit.*, pp. 67-96 for Rav Soloveitchik's analysis of the Talmudic stipulation confessions must begin with *Ana* – a prayer addressed to God.

[80] Isaiah 1:18.

[81] Psalms 51:12.

[82] See above note 72.

[83] *Sefer Likutei Amarim*, Chapter 47.

[84] Deuteronomy 10:16.

[85] Avot 3:3.

[86] Although I admire Professor George Schlesinger, I disagree with his thesis that the Argument from Design constitutes an empirical hypothesis, which accounts for the existence of the universe. (See his *Religion and Scientific Method*, Dortrecht/Boston. Freidel Publishing Co., 1977). Similarly, Professor David Weiss, an eminent scientist, also argues that the origin of the universe cannot be explained without assuming a Creator, since it would be highly improbable that chance events could result in the formation of our universe. As much as I welcome these views, which strengthen

my own religious faith, intellectual honesty compels me to point out that any other combination of occurrences would have been equally improbable. We are fully aware that many events take place against all odds. Probability exists only with respect to the state of our knowledge, but does not have any bearing upon the occurrence or non-occurrence of events, since even the most improbable events can occur at some time.

[87] See my contribution to the Commentary Symposium on "The State of Jewish Belief" *Commentary*, vol.42, number 2, August 1966.

[88] Walter Kaufmann, *Critique of Religion and Philosophy*, Garden City, Doubleday, 1961, pp.78-388.

[89] *Kuzari* I:89 and II:2.

[90] See especially, Saadiah, *The Book of Opinions and Beliefs* and Maimonides, *Guide For The Perplexed*.

[91] Chronicles I:28:9

[92] *Duties of the Heart*, I:3.

[93] Maimonides, Code, Avodat Kokhavim 1:3.

[94] Maimonides, Code, Yesodei Hatorah 1:1.

[95] B.T. Kiddushin 71a.

[96] Deuteronomy 4:29.

[97] B.T Megilah 6b.

[98] Maimonides, Code, Hilkhot Avodat Kokhavim, 1:3.

[99] A substantial part of this chapter was originally published in my article "Jewish Values and the Crisis of the Family," *New Directions in the Jewish Family and Community*, Gilbert S.

Rosenthal, (ed.) Federation of Jewish Philanthropies of New York, New York, 1974.

[100]Genesis 2:18.

[101]B.T. Sotah 17a.

[102]Nachmanides, Torah Commentary, Genesis 2:24.

[103]B.T. Yevamot 61b.

[104]Many of the formulations of this chapter are based upon my essay, "Jewish Values and the Crisis of the Family," in *New Directions in the Jewish Family and Community*, edited by Gilbert S. Rosenthal, New York, Commission on Synagogue Relations, Federation of Jewish Philanthropies of New York, 1974, pp.31-40.

[105]B.T. Menachot 93b and Bekhorot 35a.

[106]See B.T. Ketuvot 7b. The communal dimension of marriage is described in Reuven P. Bulka's *Jewish Marriage*, New York and Hoboken, Ktav Publishing House and Yeshiva University Press, 1986, p.79.

[107]B.T. Sotah 17a.

[108]Exodus 19:6.

[109]Ruth 1:16.

[110]Maimonides, Code, Hilkhot Teshuvah 3:11.

[111]Deuteronomy 32:7.

[112]See Karl Raimund Popper, *The Open Society and its Enemies*, London, Routlege, 1962.

[113]Stephen J. Pope, "'Equal Regard' versus 'Special Relations,'"

Journal of Religion, July 1997, pp.353-379.

[114]B.T. Bava Metzia 71a.

[115]Psalms 27:10.

[116]B.T. Ketuvot 68a.

[117]Job 19:26.

[118]Some parts of this chapter are based upon my "The Meaning and Significance of Jewish Survival," *Journal of Jewish Communal Service*, 11,3, Spring 1964, pp.307-316.

[119]Yehezkel Kaufmann, *Golah Veneichar*, Tel Aviv, Devir, 1929-1932, vol.1, p.190 ff.

[120]Emil L. Fackenheim, "Jewish Existence and the Living God," *Commentary*, August 1959, p.134.

[121]See Joseph B. Soloveitchik, "Kol Dodi Dofek," in *Besod Hayachid Vehayichud*, edited by Pinchas H. Peli, Jerusalem, 1976, pp.368-380.

[122]B.T. Pesachim 50b.

[123]Proverbs 1:8.

[124]B.T. Sanhedrin 74b.

[125]Exodus 20:2.

[126]Yehudah HaLevi, *Kuzari*, I:87.

[127]Commentary to Deuteronomy 32:40.

[128]Isaac Breuer, *Der Neuer Kusari: Ein Weg zum Judentum*, Frankfort, Verlag der Rabbiner Hirsch Gesellschaft, pp.73-84.

[129] B.T. Sabbath 156a; Nedarim 32a.

[130] *Op. Cit.*, p.81.

[131] Psalms 19:2.

[132] Maimonides, Code, Hilkhot Ta'aniot 1:3.

[133] See Joseph B. Soloveitchik "Kol Dodi Dofek," *op. cit.* and my "Theological Implications of the State of Israel: The Jewish View – Messianic Perspectives," *Encyclopaedia Judaica Year Book 1974*, Jerusalem, Keter Publishing House, 1974, pp.148-151.

[134] See especially verses Zechariah 8-10.

[135] See See Steven S. Schwarzschild, "The Messianic Doctrine in Contemporary Jewish Thought" *Great Jewish Ideas*, edited by Abraham Ezra Millgram, Washington, B'nai B'rith Department of Adult Jewish Education, 1964, pp.240-248.

[136] See Rav Joel Teitelbaum of Satmar, *Al Hageulah Vehatemurah* and *Encyclopaedia Judaica*, 15, pp.909-910.

[137] Isaiah 43:10.

[138] Genesis 18:25.

[139] Psalms 73:1-16.

[140] Isaiah 45:7.

[141] B.T. Berakhot 60b.

[142] Genesis Rabbah, 9:12-13.

[143] Alvin Plantinga, *God, Freedom, Evil*, Harper Torch Books, New York, Evanston, San Francisco, London, 1974.

[144] John Hick, *Evil and the God of Love*, Harper and Row, San

Francisco, 1978, p.82.

[145]Plotinus, *Enneades*, III, 2, 11. quoted by Hick, *op. cit.*, p.83.

[146]*Guide*, III, 8-14.

[147]*Religion and Scientific Method*, George Schlesinger, D. Reidel, Dordrecht, 1977.

[148]Kol Dodi Dofek, *op. cit.*

[149]My discussion of the Holocaust is largely based upon my essay, "Theological Issues Connected with Teaching the Holocaust," in *Teaching the Holocaust: An Exploration of the Problem*, Stone Saperstein Center for Jewish Education, New York, 1976, pp.24-32.

[150]*Kuzari*, II:32-40.

[151]Exodus 14:31.

[152]Habakkuk 2:4.

[153]See for example Deuteronomy 32:4; Psalms 40:11; 89:6; 92:3; 100:5; 119:90; Lamentations 3:23.

[154]B.T. Ketuvot 68a.

[155]B.T. Eruvin 69a.

[156]*Guide*, III, 51.

[157]J.T. Hagigah 1:7.

[158]B.T. Shabbat 88a.

[159]Aharon Lichtenstein, "Rav Joseph Soloveitchik," *Great Jewish Thinkers of the Twentieth Century*, edited by Simon Noveck,

B'nai B'rith Department of Adult Jewish Education, 1963, pp.296-297.

[160] J.T. Hagigah 1:7; B.T. Pesachim 50b.

[161] See the treatment of this issue in Chaim of Volozin's *Nefesh Hachaim*, 4:3-7.

[162] Avot 4:2.

[163] Maimonides, Mishnah Commentary, Avot 4:2.

[164] Deuteronomy 6:5-6.

[165] Avot 2:12.

[166] See Yitzchak Heineman, *Ta'amei Hamitzvot Besafrut Yisrael*, Jerusalem, 5719, vol.1-2.

[167] B.T. Berakhot 33b and Megillah 28a.

[168] *Guide* 3:48.

[169] Nachmanides, Torah Commentary, Deuteronomy 22:5.

[170] Eliyahu David, "Yalkut Biurei Hagra L'tenakh," *Sefer Hagra*, J.L. Maimon, ed., Jerusalem, Mosad Harav Kook, 5714, vol.2, p.253.

[171] Mosheh Sofer, *Sheelot Uteshuvot Chatam Sofer*, vol.1., Responsum 100.

[172] Sheelot Uteshuvot Chavot Yair, 67.

[173] B.T. Nazir 10a.

[174] B.T. Ta'anit 11a. See Nachmanides, Torah Commentary, Numbers 6:11.

[175]"Metahalakhic Propositions," in the *Leo Jung Jubilee Volume*, edited by Menahem M. Kasher, Norman Lamm and Leonard Rosenfeld, New York, Jewish Center, 1962, pp.211-221.

[176]Shemuel Eliezer Edels, Introduction to his Talmud Commentary and the concluding comment on tractate Yevamot.

[177]B.T. Eruvin 12b; Gittin 6b.

[178]Deuteronomy 30:12.

[179]*Ha'amek Davar*, Exodus 34:1.

[180]Sifrei, section 313 (to Deut.32:10).

[181]B.T. Gittin 60b.

[182]B.T. Berakhot 33b.

[183]William James, *The Varieties of Religious Experiences*, p.229.

[184]B.T. Berakhot 60a.

[185]Nachmanides, Torah Commentary, Leviticus 26:11. See also *Sefer Chazon Ish*. ed., S. Greineman, Jerusalem, Hamesorah, 1954, pp.64-67.

[186]Maimonides, Code, Hilkhot De'ot 4:23.

[187]Maimonides, Mishnah Commentary, Pesachim, 4:9.

[188]Psalms 136:25.

[189]Maimonides, Code, De'ot 4:33.

[190]"The Lonely Man of Faith," *Tradition*, 7,2, 1965, p.53.

[191]Psalms 127:3.

[192] B.T. Sanhedrin 96b.

[193] See Mosheh Teitelbaum, *Vayoel Mosheh*, Brooklyn, Jerusalem Publishing, 1959.

[194] Emil L. Fackenheim, *To Mend The World*, New York, Schocken Books, 1982, pp.38-58.

[195] Gershom Scholem, *The Messianic Idea in Judaism*, New York, Schocken Books, 1971, pp.35-36.

[196] Hermann Cohen, *Religion of Reason out of the Sources of Judaism*, translated with an Introduction by Simon Kaplan, New York, Frederick Unger Publishing Company, 1972, pp.236 ff.

[197] Zvi Hirsch Kalischer, *Derishath Zion*, Berlin, Louis Lamm, 1805.

[198] See Menachem M. Kasher, *Hatekufah Hagedolah*, Jerusalem, Torah Sheleimah Institute, 1968, especially pp.112-113, 140 and 502-518.

[199] *Letters of Maimonides*, translated and edited by Leon D. Stiskin, New York, Yeshiva University Press, 1977, p.120.

[200] Maimonides, Code, Hilkhot Melakhim, 11:4.

[201] For a thorough analysis of Rav Soloveitchik's position see my essay. "Hayesodot Haphilosofiim Bemishnato Hatzionit Datit shel Harav Soloveitchik," in *Enunah bisemanim mishtanim*, Avi Sagi ed., Jerusalem, Department of Torah Education and Culture, 1996, pp.111-122.

[202] *Halakhic Man*, p.100.

[203] "Redemption, Prayer, Talmud Torah," *Tradition*, 17,2, Spring 1978, p.55.

[204] Joseph B.Soloveitchik, *Divrei Hashkaphah*, Jerusalem, Department of Torah Education and Culture, World Zionist Organization, 5752, pp.241-242.

[205] Saadiah, *op. cit.*, chapter 10.

[206] Ecclesiastes 1:2.

[207] See my *Ethics of Responsibility*, *op. cit*, Chapter 6.

[208] B.T. Sanhedrin 89a.

[209] Avot 5:1.

[210] B.T. Shabbat 55a.

[211] Bereshit Rabbah 68.

[212] B.T. Eruvin 13b; Gittin 6b.

[213] Avot 5:17.

[214] Abraham R.Besdin, *Reflections of the Rav,* Hoboken, Ktav, 1993, pp.51-70.

[215] Ben Zion Bokser. *The Road to Renewal*, *Tradition*, 13,3, Winter 1972, pp.147-148.

[216] *A Social and Religious Story of the Jews*, Columbia University Press, 1958, p.12.

[217] *Two Essays on Zionism and Judaism*, by Ahad Ha-am, translated from the Hebrew by Leon Simon, London, George Routledge and Sons, 1922, pp.8-14.

[218] *Ibid.*

[219] *Op. Cit.*, p10.

[220] *Ibid.*

[221] *Ibid.*

[222] Genesis 18:25.

[223] Kings I. 8:41-42.

[224] *Ibid.* 8:60.

[225] Isaiah 2:3.

[226] Avot 3:4.

[227] *Ibid.*

[228] B.T. Gittin 61a.

[229] See my *Ethics of Responsibility*, pp.50-52 and my essay, "Darkhei Shalom," in *Gesher*, 1978, pp.80-86.

[230] *Ibid.*, p118.

[231] See Rav Nissim's Introduction to Talmud.

[232] Ezekiel 46:49.

[233] B.T. Kiddushin 30b.

[234] See Rashi Commentary to Exodus 24:12.

[235] See Peter Singer, "Famine Affluence and Morality." *Philosophy and Public Affairs*, 1,3, pp.229-243.

[236] B.T. Bava Metzia 71a.

[237] Hermann Cohen, *Die Religion der Vernunft aus den Quellen des Judentums*, Frankfort, J. Kaufmann, pp.348 ff.

Sources And Bibliography

[238] Jeremiah 29:7.

[239] Pirkei De'Rabbi Eleazar 10.

[240] Meckhilta Bo 12; Pirkei Derabbi Elazar 10.

[241] A considerable part of this chapter is excerpted from my essay, "Pluralism and the Halakhah," *Tradition*, Spring 1962.

[242] Proverbs 3:6.

[243] B.T. Berakhot 63a.

[244] B.T. Ketuvot 66b.

[245] Friedrich Nietzsche, *The Genealogy of Morals*, New York, Doubleday, 1956. Cf. also *Also sprach Zarathustra*, Lepzig, Kroner, 1918, pp.88-90 and pp.127-130.

[246] B.T. Bava Batra 10b.

[247] B.T. Pesachim 50b and Nazir 23b.

[248] *Ibid.*

[249] See *Nefesh Hachaim*, Appendage to Part 3, Chapter 3.

[250] The bulk of this chapter is excerpted from my "A Jewish Theology and Philosophy of the Sabbath," in *The Sabbath in Jewish and Christian Tradition*, Tamara C. Eskenazi, Daniel J. Harrimgtom S.J. and William H. Shea (eds.), Crossroad, New York, 1991.

[251] Midrash Tehillim on Psalm 92:1.

[252] B.T. Rosh Hashanah 27a.

[253] Deuteronomy 8:17.

[254]*Ibid.* 18:18.

[255]Isaiah 57:13.

[256]B.T. Shabbat 10b.

[257]Isaiah 56:2 and 58:13-14.

[258]Nehemiah 9:14.

[259]B.T. Shabbat 19a.

[260]Eric Fromm, *The Forgotten Language*, New York, Grove Press. 1985, pp.488-491.

[261]*Avot De' Rabbi Natan*, 11:1.

[262]Abraham Isaac Kook, *Olat Raayah*, Jerusalem, 5709, vol.2, p.146.

[263]Isaiah 58:14.

[264]B.T. Shabbat 57b.

[265]Isaiah 58:6-14.

[266]Yehudah HaLevi, *Kuzari*, 2:48.

[267]*Ibid.*, 2:50; 3:23.

[268]Maimonides, *Guide*, III, 27.

[269]Walter S. Wurzburger, *op. cit.*, chapter 3.

[270]Joseph B. Soloveitchik. "Uvikashtem" in *Ish Hahalakhah Galui Venistar*. Jerusalem, World Zionist Organization, 1978, pp.180-186.

[271] *Netivot Olam*, "Netiv Gemilut Chassadim," chapter 1.

[272] For an interesting treatment of the doctrine that ethics calls for the cultivation of moral perceptions as to the needs of individuals, see Lawrence A. Bloom's *Moral Perception and Particularity*, Cambridge University Press, New York, 1994.

[273] Maimonides, Mishnah Commentary, Avot 2:5.

[274] A similar observation is made by R.Loew in his *Gur Aryeh al Hatorah*, at the end of his commentary on *Parshat Yitro*.

[275] B.T. Kiddushin 31a.

[276] Yechiel Mikhel Epstein, *Sefer Arukh Hashulchan*, Yorah Deah, 240,1-3.

[277] Avot 5:23.

[278] Maimonides. Mishnah Commentary, "Eight Chapters," Chapter 6.

[279] Maimonides, Code, Hilkhot Deot, 1:5.

[280] Maimonides, Code, Hilkhot Teshuvah, 7:3.

[281] Maimonides, Code, Hilkhot Deot, 1:6.

[282] Deuteronomy 28:10.

[283] Avot 2:16.

[284] Genesis Rabbah, 100:1.

[285] B.T. Sotah 22b.

[286] B.T. Berakhot 64a.

[287] Psalm 105:3.

[288] Maimonides, Code, Hilkhot Yesodei Hatorah, 1:1-5.

[289] Alfred Kazin, *A Walker in the City*, New York, Harcourt, Brace and Company, 1951, p.46.

[290] Lamentations 3:23.

[291] B.T. Chagigah 14a.

[292] Quoted by Walter Kaufmann, in *From Shakespeare to Existentialism*, New York, World Publishing Company, 1956, p.195.

[293] Exodus 15:2.